Tikal Report No. 23D

MISCELLANEOUS INVESTIGATIONS IN CENTRAL TIKAL: STRUCTURES IN AND AROUND THE LOST WORLD PLAZA

University Museum Monograph 148

Tikal Report No. 23D

MISCELLANEOUS INVESTIGATIONS IN CENTRAL TIKAL: STRUCTURES IN AND AROUND THE LOST WORLD PLAZA

H. Stanley Loten

Series Editors
William A. Haviland
Simon Martin

Published by

UNIVERSITY OF PENNSYLVANIA MUSEUM
of Archaeology and Anthropology
Philadelphia
2018

CATALOGING-IN-PUBLICATION DATA IS ON FILE WITH THE LIBRARY OF CONGRESS

ISBN 13: 978-1-934536-97-1
ISBN 10: 1-934536-97-0

© 2018 by the University of Pennsylvania Museum of Archaeology and Anthropology
Philadelphia, PA
All rights reserved. Published 2018

Distributed for the University of Pennsylvania Museum of Archaeology and Anthropology
by the University of Pennsylvania Press.

Printed in the United States of America on acid-free paper.

Table of Contents

LIST OF TABLES.......................................vii

LIST OF ILLUSTRATIONS..............................ix

EDITORS' NOTE..xi

ABBREVIATIONS......................................xiii

SELECTED ARCHITECTURAL TERMS....................xv

1 INTRODUCTION.....................................1

2 STRUCTURE 5C-49..................................3

3 STRUCTURE 5D-77..................................9

4 STRUCTURE 5D-84..................................13

5 STRUCTURE 5D-86..................................17

6 STRUCTURE 5D-87..................................23

7 STRUCTURE 6D-1...................................29

8 CONCLUSIONS.....................................33

REFERENCES..35

ILLUSTRATIONS.......................................37

Tables

Table 2.1	Structure 5C-49: Room Areas	4
Table 2.2	Structure 5C-49: Face Dimensions of Wall-Facing Stones	4
Table 2.3	Structure 5C-49: Face Dimensions of Vault-Soffit Facing Stones	6
Table 2.4	Structure 5C-49: Time Spans	8
Table 3.1	Structure 5D-77: Face Dimensions of Wall-Facing Stretchers	10
Table 3.2	Structure 5D-77: Vault-Soffit Facing-Stone Dimensions	11
Table 3.3	Structure 5D-77: Time Spans	12
Table 4.1	Structure 5D-84: Time Spans	15
Table 5.1	Structure 5D-86: Wall-Facing Stone Dimensions	18
Table 5.2	Structure 5D-86: Inset Panel Dimensions	19
Table 5.3	Structure 5D-86: Face Dimensions of Vault-Soffit Stones	20
Table 5.4	Structure 5D-86: Time Spans	22
Table 6.1	Structure 5D-87: Vault-Beam Sockets in Room 2	25
Table 6.2	Structure 5D-87: Face Dimensions of Vault-Soffit Headers	25
Table 6.3	Structure 5D-87: Time Spans	27
Table 7.1	Structure 6D-1: Face Dimensions of Exterior Wall Stretchers	30
Table 7.2	Structure 6D-1: Time Spans	31

Illustrations

Figure 1	Structure 5C-49 Location and Photograph
Figure 2	Structure 5C-49 Plan
Figure 3	Structure 5C-49 Building Plan
Figure 4	Structure 5C-49 Details
Figure 5	Structure 5C-49 Superstructure
Figure 6	Structure 5C-49 Roof Structure
Figure 7	Structure 5C-49 Section/Profile B-B'
Figure 8	Structure 5C-49 Problematical Deposit 181
Figure 9	Structure 5C-49 Problematical Deposit 181 and 182
Figure 10	Structure 5C-49 Roof-Structure Plan
Figure 11	Structure 5C-49 Section/Profile A-A'
Figure 12	Structure 5C-49 Problematical Deposit 182
Figure 13	Structure 5D-77 Location and Photograph
Figure 14	Structure 5D-77 Plan and Section
Figure 15	Structure 5D-77 Section/Profile B-B'
Figure 16	Structure 5D-84 Location and Plan
Figure 17	Structure 5D-84 Section/Profile A-A'
Figure 18	Structure 5D-86 Location
Figure 19	Structure 5D-86 Photographs
Figure 20	Structure 5D-86 Room 2 Vault
Figure 21	Structure 5D-86 Photographs
Figure 22	Structure 5D-86 Plan
Figure 23	Structure 5D-86 Section/Profile A-A'
Figure 24	Structure 5D-86 Building Plan
Figure 25	Structure 5D-86 Stucco Modeling
Figure 26	Structure 5D-86 Stucco Modeling
Figure 27	Structure 5D-87 Location and Perspective
Figure 28	Structure 5D-87 Plan
Figure 29	Structure 5D-87 Section/Profile A-A'
Figure 30	Structure 5D-87 North Elevation
Figure 31	Structure 5D-87 Details
Figure 32	Structure 5D-87 Section/Profile B-B'
Figure 33	Structure 5D-87 Section/Profile C-C'
Figure 34	Structure 5D-87 Building Plan

Figure 35   Structure 6D-1 Location and Plan
Figure 36   Structure 6D-1 Section/Profile A-A'

Editors' Note

Tikal Reports present the results of the University of Pennsylvania excavations from 1956–1969, largely in accord with the projected scheme set out by William R. Coe and William A. Haviland in Tikal Report 12. A great deal of research has taken place at Tikal since those investigations were completed with, in particular, several important projects undertaken by the Instituto Nacional de Antropología e Historia de Guatemala and the Agencia Española de Cooperación Internacional. Since their work has often enlarged upon that conducted by the University of Pennsylvania,—in some cases excavating the same structures—there is a clear opportunity to integrate recent and historical investigations to produce a synthetic treatment. This idea is undoubtedly appealing, but it is one we have resisted for the monograph series. The reasons are threefold. Firstly, consistency of scope and presentation was integral to the original scheme and has been implemented in all the reports published thus far. Secondly, the Tikal Report authors do not have access to the newly produced data to anything like the extent necessary to do that work justice. Thirdly, to produce synthetic treatments of this kind would introduce very considerable delays in publishing future Tikal Reports, hampering the work of those scholars and students who could make immediate use of the data they contain. In acknowledgment of subsequent work, the introduction to each volume in the series will henceforth note where later work has taken place on the same structures and reference the relevant publications. Even without the addition of new data, the Tikal Report series provides needed information on things that can no longer be observed first hand, either because of excavation or continuing destruction by the elements.

William A. Haviland
Simon Martin
Series Editors

Abbreviations

Bm.: Beam
Chm.: Chamber
Dr.: Door/Doorway
E: East
Fl.: Floor
I.P.: Inset Panel
N: North
PD.: Problematical Deposit
Rm.: Room
S: South
Str.: Structure
VB.: Vault Beam
W: West

Selected Architectural Terms

Note: These are just a few terms that occur in this volume. Some are new, others perhaps just not in general use in the Tikal series.

Aggregate
In concrete small stones or gravel are essential as stuff that the cement can stick to. Without aggregate concrete is mere grout with little strength as a mass.

Basal Platform
A substructure body exclusively sustaining a lower substructure platform.

Batter
Non-vertical faces are battered. Leaning outward is negative batter, inward is positive.

Beam
A spanning member is a beam. Wood beams are common but stone ones are known, particularly as lintels.

Building
The part of a structure that stands on a building platform and contains accessible rooms.

Building Platform
A building platform anticipates the plan of the building and provides a basis for the walls (see also "Fake Building Platform," below).

Butt
The parts of beams that bear on their supports are their butts. Some butts are concealed, others exposed.

Capstone
Stones bridging the gap between half-vaults are capstones. Wood members bridging half-vault gaps are known and may be described as wooden capstones.

Construction Stage
Major works of architecture at Tikal display a standard set of the following features: basal platform, pyramid, lower substructure platform, supplementary platform, building platform, building, and, roofcomb. Building and building platform appear most frequently, and others appear on various structures in various combinations. They are numbered from topmost to basal, but described in reverse order, that is, basal to topmost. Although the terms imply distinct stages of construction, this is not always the case. For example, some building platforms are not stages of construction at all, and many buildings present walls, vaults, and upper zones as distinct constructional modules that perhaps might best be designated as substages, though this has not been formalized.

Cord Holder
Recessed pegs to which cords could be tied, usually found in interior wall faces flanking doorway openings, often in sets of four.

Epicentral Tikal
This term refers to the parts of the city center that are interconnected by continuous plaster paving. The six structures described in this volume are all within it. Individual location maps for each structure depict part of it. By means of the causeway system, the epicenter extends from the Great Plaza to the North

Group and to Great Temple VI. Since plaster paving is inherently fragile, maintaining such an extensive paving must have been important and meaningful.

Fake Building Platform
Beginning in Middle Classic times at Tikal, and evident only in certain structures, the building platform is no more than a series of moldings at the foot of exterior building wall faces. In some cases, this is obvious; in others, the building platform image is entirely convincing and requires excavation to show its true nature. It may be that many Late Classic Tikal structures display apparent building platforms that appear to support walls, but in fact are no more than exterior facade treatments.

Falsework
A timber structure set up during construction to establish lines, angles, and heights. Evidence consists only of socket holes.

Half-vault
From Intermediate through the Late Classic at Tikal vaults were installed by halves, first on one side of a room and then for completion, on the other side. The two half-vaults do not touch or lean against each other; each is independently stable. Short end-vault units prevent the long half-vaults from rolling into the room space.

Header
A facing stone set with its length projecting into the hearting of the wall or other feature.

Jamb
The sides of doorway openings are called jambs.

Lintel
A beam over a doorway, window, or niche is a lintel beam. Most lintels at Tikal employ a number of beams, many seemingly much too small in diameter for the load imposed by the vault mass and they must have been braced until vault mortar had reached full set.

Lower Substructure Platform
A number of structures consist of a building, a building platform, and a lower substructure platform that does not conform to definitions for supplementary platforms, pyramids, or basal platforms. These are designated simply as lower substructure platforms.

Medial Molding
At wall-top level a corbel course projecting out over the exterior wall surface is known as a medial molding.

Outset
Terraces, walls, and roofcombs, often have elements of surface projected out from other elements. Some may have iconographic significance, particularly rear axial outsets and stair-side outsets. Even side outsets might have carried meanings that would have been known to the people using the structures.

Preplastered
Workers sometimes applied plaster to masonry units prior to setting them in place. This is seen only on capstones in Late Classic construction and hence they provide a reliable diagnostic to this era at Tikal.

Range
Rooms of a building arranged with their length perpendicular to the structure axis constitute a "range." This is the basis of the term "range-type structure." Some range-type structures have more than one range set one in front of the other.

Rear Axial Outset
Certain structures have axial outsets in their rear facades, designated as rear axial outsets. These do not appear to serve any structural function and are not accessible as ledges on which persons might stand. They seem to have some significance in themselves, and they correlate with a definite set of other architectural features that may define temples.

Return Face
This term applies to facets of exterior surface that run perpendicular to the general orientation of facades—for example, end elements of outsets.

Roofcomb
A superstructure body, not supplied with accessible rooms, erected on a roof.

Socket
The hole left by a rotted out beam is a socket.

Soffit
The under-surface of a projecting member is its soffit. Vault surfaces over a room are soffit surfaces.

Spall
Small stones that occur in masonry joints and beds are spalls. Some may have been placed so as to provide a correct setting for the blocks, others may have been included in the mortar.

Stair-side Outset
Terrace outsets flanking stairs are known as stair-side outsets.

Stair-side Ramp
Some outset stairs present sheer edges, while others have a slightly raised ramp-like edge, also known by the terms "*alfarda*" and balustrade.

Standing Architecture
Tikal ruins include many architectural structures only partially collapsed. Project operations cleared debris away from many of these but others were left as originally found. These are known as examples of standing architecture and were recorded without removal of collapsed material or vegetation.

Stretcher
A facing stone set with its length running in the plane of the surface.

Subapron
Apron profiles at Tikal are of two main types: two-element aprons and three-element aprons. The two-element type typifies Early Classic work and consists of an upper part projecting over a lower part; the lower part is the subapron. This implies that the upper part is the apron, although the term "apron" is also applied to the whole feature whether two element or three element. In three-element aprons the subapron is the middle part.

Substructure
The parts below the building are known collectively as the substructure.

Supplementary Platform
A substructure body intervening between a lower substructure platform and a building platform.

Upper Zone
The exterior element corresponding to the vaults and overhanging exterior wall faces is the upper zone.

Vault
Masonry constructions that span over rooms or chambers are vaults. The vaults at Tikal are unlike arches in that one side does not depend on the other, they do not exert lateral thrusts, and do not require buttresses.

Vault-back
Some vaults have outer surfaces underlying upper zone material; these are known as vault-back surfaces. Some vaults at Tikal do not have vault-backs but most do.

Vault Beam
All known vaults at Tikal contain either wood beams, beam butts, or beam sockets. The beams are known as vault beams and in many cases were installed prior to masonry work as part of falsework and/or formwork. The way that vault soffit stones were cut around beams shows that the beams were in place first.

Veneer Facings
Facing stones proportioned so that their height is distinctly greater than their thickness are known as veneer stones.

Wall
Elements installed to define rooms are designated as walls. Surfaces of platforms are not referred to as walls, but as faces.

Wall Top
In Late Classic work at Tikal, masons completed wall construction by plastering inside and out and across the top of the walls. Wall-top plaster is a reliable diagnostic of Late Classic construction at Tikal.

I

Introduction

The Structures that are described in this volume (5C-49, 5D-77, 5D-84, 5D-86, 5D-87, and 6D-1) are found in and around the so-called Lost World Plaza and they belong to the Tikal Project category "Standing Architecture." That is, though partially collapsed to various degrees, some features still remain in place and accessible without excavation. In the Tikal Project base maps (TR. 11), these structures are hatched.

These structures were recorded within the same architectural surface survey as those described in TR. 23A, 23B, and 23C. In the measuring process, the trees and bushes growing on them were disturbed as little as possible—their roots often were the only things holding back still further collapse.

The plans, sections, and elevations describing these structures present extant material in solid line, whereas broken line indicates hidden features concealed by debris but hinted at by debris contours. Such unseen features must be understood as guesswork, though some aspects are probably reliable. For example, substructure heights may be accurate while details of terraces, stairs, and outsets, shown in broken line, might be quite wrong.

Broken line also depicts fallen features by extension based on surviving accessible fragments. The volume of collapse debris often provides clues for such things as heights of roofcombs, though the precise line remains merely an estimate. All standing structures at Tikal have vaulted buildings, though most vaults have now collapsed—sometimes leaving fragments standing near the ends of rooms—while others remain almost fully in place over rooms one can walk into. Deterioration of wooden lintels has been responsible for much loss of vaulting.

The plaster finish rarely survives on surfaces standing above debris, yet traces often remain under projecting moldings. From these scraps, it is clear that all masonry surfaces were originally plastered. When freshly applied, plaster would have greatly altered the impression we now have from the exposed stonework. Structures that now appear dark were originally shiny and perhaps even brilliant in sunlight. Removal of the trees that surround and even cover structures standing in the forest would also greatly change our impressions, particularly of rooms, which now seem dark, dank, and moldy. All the structures described here once were surrounded by plaster paving or at least face onto plastered plazas and courts. Light levels would have been much higher and the rooms would not have been so dark.

Structure reports are organized by standard construction stages: basal platform, lower substructure platform, supplementary platform, building platform, building, and roofcomb. Tikal Project conventions assume these to be real units of construction and, in most cases, they are, but not always. In particular, some building platforms are nothing more than moldings applied to exterior wall faces and, in terms of construction, belong with wall features. This distinction, however, is ignored here to keep the descriptions of these building platforms consistently formatted, but their atypical construction is discussed in the text. Some such features are designated fake building platforms.

If Maya builders at Tikal actually did think of some architectural features as fakes, this may mean that these features conveyed some sort of significance by their external appearance, that is, as iconic forms. In the case of fake building platforms, their iconography may relate to residential construction or house platforms, which have long-standing provenance.

Subsequent to the excavations of the Tikal Project, work at the site has continued. Some of the structures covered in this volume have undergone further investigation and are presented in the work of Laporte and Fialko (1995). Where relevant, these data are referenced in the text.

II

Structure 5C-49

Structure 5C-49 (Fig. 1b) is located at the SW quadrant of the site center (Fig. 1a). An arrangement of debris mounds resembling a small causeway leads from the S into the epicentral complex of monumental structures connected by paved plaza surfaces (TR. 11:Perdido and Temple IV sheets). The structure faces S toward this seemingly formalized entry point. The rear part of the superstructure stands with vaults intact W of the centerline. Everything else is either fallen or obscured beneath collapse debris. Cardinal orientation, taken from the rear exterior wall, runs 2.5° S of E (magnetic), that is, approximately 8° E of true N as determined for the TR. 11 maps.

Loten recorded 5C-49 in the summer of 1966 under the Tikal Standing Architectural Survey Program, a surface survey of standing architecture. Structures investigated in this program are those presenting enough architectural details for a reasonably complete picture with minimal excavation. Structure 5C-49 provides this at superstructure level, but the substructure remains largely unknown.

Both Maler and Tozzer mention 5C-49. It appears in the Tozzer/Merwin 1911 map as number 67. Maler (1911:55) thought the rear part of the building was solid and that it had only two rooms. Tozzer (1911:126) noted the presence of three rooms, but considered the structure "unimportant."

Construction Stages

Three construction stages are evident. A hard plaster surface marks the top of the lower substructure platform. This indicates completion of this part of the structure before work commenced on upper parts. The only other pause-line is that of the building roof underlying the roof structure. The three construction stages identified are the lower substructure platform, the building, and the roof structure.

Lower Substructure Platform, Building Platform and Building, and Building Walls

LOWER SUBSTRUCTURE PLATFORM

Broken lines representing this part of the structure are estimates based on debris profiles. Details such as the number of terraces and outsets are not available (Fig. 2, 3). The large fully projecting stair is evident in debris profiles. Minor clearing exposed one step (Fig. 4a) and the E stair-side ramp. Total height is approximately 17 m. Absent earlier structures within the fabric, the volume of masonry is approximately 14,000 m^3, with the stair alone representing 1,870 m^3. The top surface is Fl. 5, a hard, smooth plaster topping at the W side inset, but rougher where examined along the N facade.

Investigations subsequent to the Tikal Project have revealed the presence of earlier versions of 5C-49, amounting to about three-quarters the apparent volume of the lower substructure platform (Laporte and Fialko 1995:fig. 38). From these data, the volume of masonry employed for the final version of the substructure is about 5,400 m^3.

BUILDING PLATFORM AND BUILDING

These two parts of the structure appear to have been installed as part the same construction stage. Therefore, they are classified as subcomponents.

Only a very small remnant of masonry, representing building platform material, is visible at the W side inset (Fig. 5a). Clearly, this is a fake building platform. None of its material actually sustains the walls. It is an exterior application of facade elements that do not sustain any superior elements. No surface profiles are visible. At the front, some may exist beneath debris. At the rear, none remain in place. The rear top level roughly corresponds with Fl. 1 in Rm. 3 (Fig. 5a). This level is extrapolated from the W side inset where it is higher than the Rm. 2 floor. The front part no doubt corresponds with the floor level in Rm. 1. If it did not, there would be a strange condition at the doorway(s). Total masonry volume might be about 20 m³.

BUILDING WALLS

Walls of the building stand on Fl. 5, the top surface of the lower substructure platform (Fig. 7). Since the fake building platform is laid up against the walls, they are higher than they appear in elevation (Fig. 5b). Room floors were installed on top of material built up inside the walls on top of Fl. 5.

Plan configuration of walls includes side insets but no evident rear axial outset. A three-room plan is assumed (Fig. 3), although only the rear two are actually visible above collapse debris. The facade formation, projecting a frontal part and a rear part, results directly from the room arrangement. That is, exterior form at wall level is not considered as a mere facade convention even though that appears to be the case at the building platform level.

From debris contours, the front room appears much wider than the other two and projects laterally well beyond the rear wall lines (Table 2.1).

TABLE 2.1
Structure 5C-49: Room Areas

Room	Area (m²)	Width-to-Length Proportion
1	40 (±)	1:4.3 (±)
2	15.4	1:6.8
3	14.7	1:7.5

Wall thicknesses vary at different locations around the building: 0.70, 1.0, 1.30, and 2 m. Apart from the "thick" wall between Rm. 1 and 2, all walls can be characterized as "thin." Thickness-to-height ratios vary as 1:6.3, 1:4.4, 1:3.5, and 1:2.2.

For exterior wall facings, masons employed roughly shaped flat-slab stones minimally dressed on the face. Distinction between headers and stretchers is not evident.

Although facing stones are bedded horizontally, course levels cannot be followed for any distance. Mortar joints are thick and spalls absent. Interior facing stones are slightly smaller than exterior stones and wall surfaces are more undulating. Relatively high values for standard deviation (Table 2.2) indicate that masons did not employ a standard unit dimension. Despite uneven wall faces, all walls are essentially vertical.

TABLE 2.2
Structure 5C-49: Face Dimensions of Wall-Facing Stones

Dimension	n	Mean (m)	Standard Deviation	Range (m)
Exterior Length	100	0.31	8.15	0.15–0.57
Exterior Height	100	0.11	3.61	0.05–0.20
Interior Length	40	0.23	5.53	0.11–0.33
Interior Height	40	0.10	2.44	0.06–0.17

Interior wall faces retain a single thick, soft coat of dark gray plaster undulating irregularly over facing stones. All exterior plaster has vanished except for remnants of two thick coats on the rear wall (Fig. 3, 5a:1). The inner coat is 0.10 m thick, smoothly finished, with vertical grooves about 0.65 m apart. The outer coat (Fig. 5a:1), also about 0.10 m thick, repeats the vertical grooves. Extant fragments include two grooves near the W end of the wall and just under the medial molding. Grooved plaster, or perhaps more correctly "stucco," may have extended over all exterior walls or may have been confined to the rear wall. There does not appear to be a plaster coat underlying the grooved stucco layers. No traces of paint remain.

Wall-core masonry employs small-stone rubble with occasional inclusions of larger slabs similar to facing stones. The core matrix is a tight gray mortar of good adhesive quality similar to the mortar used at wall faces.

The W wall of Rm. 2 presents a well-finished, rectangular opening, 0.37 m high by 0.48 m wide, which looks like a window, but at 1.85 m above the floor it is well above average ancient Maya eye-level (Fig. 5b). Sill and jamb surfaces are fully plastered. Three subrectangular stone slabs about 0.18 m thick span the opening. In view of its height, it may have been installed as a vent, but if so, one might expect a similar opening in the E wall. The W location would serve to admit low-angle solar rays at certain times of the year. This could have motivated construction of the opening.

A lintel of three large semi-rounded wooden beams spanned the doorway opening to Rm. 3 (Fig. 5a:2–4). The beams rested on unplastered lintel beds that had been renewed secondarily, together with secondary jambs that reduced the doorway width when open. If the original lintel beams had failed, secondary jamb units may have been installed as expedients for installation of new (larger?) lintel beams. A fragment of *Tzapote* wood in debris near this doorway may be from these replacement lintel beams. Plaster of the secondary jamb units is similar to primary plaster in thickness and undulating surface, but is white rather than gray.

The primary floor of Rm. 3 appears to be Fl. 4 (Fig. 8a). On this, three secondary floors have been installed. Floor 1 is composed of 3 cm of thick, soft, white marly plaster, worn and eroded. Floor 2, 3 cm thick, consists of hard, smooth, white plaster not worn where exposed in the W part of Rm. 3. Floor 3 may be a relatively well-finished subfloor preparatory to installation of Fl. 2, raising the floor level of Rm. 3 by 4 cm (Fig. 9a,b). Core material under Fl. 3 includes slabs similar to wall-facing units.

Two caches have been intruded through Fl. 1; these are discussed below (see "Special Deposits").

The bench that occupies the center of Rm. 3 and either blocks or partially fills the doorway has been installed on Fl. 1 and, thus, is by several removes secondary to the building. Above it is a niche secondarily installed in the wall, plastered, and then subsequently filled with stones.

Two primary cord holders are visible in the S wall of Rm. 3 flanking the doorway (Fig. 4b). Both are unusual types. One has a diagonal stone bar as the tie rod and the other has a vertical hole drilled in a stone slab.

A horizontal bedding surface of mortar can be seen at the rear and at the W side inset. This constitutes a sort of wall top but it is not plastered. It does not represent a significant pause following completion of wall construction. The grooved stucco applications on the rear wall could not have been installed prior to the medial molding. The mortar "wall top" probably represents a leveling operation meant to establish a bedding plane for the medial molding rather than a pause in the construction process.

Volume of masonry employed for walls amounts to approximately 250 m^3.

Vaulting

Extant vaulting can be seen over the W half of Rm. 2 and 3. Spring outsets vary from 0.08 to 0.20 m, set roughly two courses above the medial moldings. Soffit profiles vary irregularly, undulating from concave to convex at various points. Soffit angles between vault top and spring (that is, ignoring profiles) are 25.5° in Rm. 3 and 23° in Rm. 2. The soffit angle in Rm. 1 would have to be very much flatter, roughly 45°, an angle that must approach the limit of viable ancient Maya vaulting and probably contributed to the complete collapse of this part of the building. End-vault-soffit angles in Rm. 2 and 3 are similar to half-vault angles in the same rooms.

Soffit facers are predominantly headers but include some stones that cannot be classified as either. Coursing runs for short stretches, but generally the two vaults can be considered as seven courses high. Face shapes are roughly rectangular with the greater dimension most frequently in the vertical (Table 2.3).

Half-vault and end-vault facings are essentially identical. In both units, dimensional standardization is relatively low. Face-to-butt lengths vary greatly around a mean value of 0.38 m with a standard deviation of 14.31 for a sample of 14 stones.

Capstones are preplastered, but not standardized for either shape or size. This indicates that vault soffits were plastered prior to capstone installation. In "late" construction, preplastered capstones are accompanied by vault-back surfaces. Here, no vault-back could be identified and root penetration had reached the butts of the soffit stones (Fig. 6b). This implies either absence of a vault-back or an unplastered vault-back.

Vault beams in Rm. 3 are in two levels except for one extra beam at the W end (Fig. 9b). Three surviving beam stubs are uncarved logwood (Fig. 9b:1–3). Diameters range from 0.09 to 0.15 m; depths are from 0.74 to 0.90 m. An exception is Bm. 7, which passes right through the surviving vault mass. The beam housed in Socket 5 was forked 0.53 m in from the soffit surface. Sockets 7 and 8 run at an angle into the vault mass. The beams employed may have been somewhat crooked. Whether beams were set in place prior to installation of vault masonry is unclear. Roughly shaped soffit stones fail to reveal the sequence of installation.

A plaster surface is visible above the doorway to Rm. 3. It slopes upward toward the rear and is badly damaged by root action. This appears to be a roof surface indicating a formal pause-line between building construction and roof-structure work (Fig. 6a).

Upper Zones and Roof

The only extant upper-zone surface masonry is located near the center of the rear facade (Fig. 1b). Medial molding corbels remain across the rear and at the W side inset (Fig. 7). A sculptural panel may exist near center on the rear upper zone but it is greatly root damaged and problematic. The rear upper zone probably has a plain profile and frontal profiles are not extant.

The total volume of masonry in vaults and upper zones amounts to about 240 m^3.

A vaulted chamber exists above the roof. Visible roof plaster, though damaged, shows no signs of weathering (Fig. 6a). Therefore, the roof structure is probably a primary feature and is only 1.5 m high. Its top surface is level and it may never have been any higher. Thanks to vault failure the chamber is now accessible, but originally it was probably not so.

In plan, the chamber is complex (Fig. 10), the middle part wider than the two ends. Such elaboration of interior space does not appear consistent with intent to reduce the weight of material. The chamber may be present for some other reason.

The vault springs from roof level (Fig. 6a). There is no sign of a floor surface. Soffit profiles undulate irregularly and retain no traces of plaster. Exterior

TABLE 2.3
Structure 5C-49: Face Dimensions of Vault-Soffit Facing Stones

Dimension	n	Mean (m)	Standard Deviation	Range (m)
Half-Vault Length	40	0.15	5.48	0.07–0.28
Half-Vault Height	40	0.29	6.97	0.12–0.47
End-Vault Length	19	0.16	3.10	0.09–0.23
End-Vault Height	19	0.29	5.35	0.20–0.40

faces appear plain with no sign of any sculptural treatment. This certainly is not a roofcomb designed to increase the apparent height of the structure and for display of sculptural motifs. The chamber may be the sole aspect for which the term "roofcomb" may be appropriate.

The volume of masonry needed for the roof structure totals approximately 75 m³.

Architecture

Category names such as "Great Temple," "Pyramid Temple," or "Pyramidal Structure" are the labels that eventually will apply to a fully excavated 5C-49. The lower substructure platform, approximately 17 m high, places the structure in some such category (Fig. 11). Absence of a rear axial outset and the possibility of vertical grooves on exterior walls will appear as anomalous features. A subcategory may be defined by presence of stair-side ramps or *alfardas* on the main stair.

Attributes of wall and vault construction indicate an "early" date. Presence of preplastered capstones implies a "late" position. Perhaps 5C-49 is a work of the Middle Classic Period.

The fake building platform presents another attribute rarely identified, but possibly quite common during the Late Classic at Tikal. Even more unusual is the apparent two-level building platform applied to a structure with three rooms stepping up from front to rear.

Finally, the stumpy roof structure presents another feature that may place 5C-49 in a class by itself among Tikal structures.

Special Deposits

Removal of a thin layer of debris in the W half of Rm. 3 disclosed two floor patches, each accompanied by open looter holes (Fig. 3, 8b, 9a,b, 12a,b). On-floor debris included fine-grained material (plaster melt?), animal bones, some human bone fragments, a censor fragment, and vessel fragments that fit the reconstructible vessel in the PD. 181 looter pit (Cat. 120A-4, 5, 18).

The patches, sealing cuts through Fl. 1, were left undisturbed. The looter holes were cleaned out and their contents examined. It appeared that the patches had sealed caches made while the building was still being used. Due to looter disturbance, the original deposits are classified as problematical deposits. The patches sealing them are well made, though not smoothly finished.

Problematical Deposit 181

LOCATION

Structure 5C-49, Rm. 3, W half: about halfway between the W wall and the axial bench, roughly in the middle of the room width.

CONTENT AND ARRANGEMENT

The floor patch has two courses of horizontally bedded stones that span the hole cut for the deposit. The top surface of this patch is somewhat smoother than the PD. 182 patch and does not project quite so far above Fl. 1.

The looter pit W of PD. 181 (Fig. 9a,b) had been partially refilled. It contained a reconstructible vessel (Cat. 120A-2) inverted over some unworked animal bone (Cat. 120A-3u). Material beneath the vessel included charcoal, obsidian, unworked bird, rodent, and bat bones, one animal tooth, and a human infant skeleton (Cat. 120A-9 through 13). The original cut that was not impacted by the looter's pit retained charcoal, a flint flake, a retouched obsidian blade, and unworked human and animal bones (Cat. 120A-14 through 17).

DISCUSSION

The reconstructible vessel (above) seems to have been deliberately placed in the looter hole. Looters may have done this as a gesture intended to avert any evil effects of their looting. This may imply that the looters retained the beliefs that motivated the original deposits.

Problematical Deposit 182

LOCATION

Structure 5C-49, in the SW corner of Rm. 3.

CONTENT AND ARRANGEMENT

The patch is of good-quality mortar with small

stone aggregate. The looter pit contained collapse debris, vessel fragments fitting others from above Fl. 1, and mixed human and animal skeletal material (Cat. 120A-1, 18). The original cut that was not impacted by the looter's pit contained a mix of material similar to that found in PD. 181 (Cat. 120A-6 through 8).

DISCUSSION

The original deposits had been thoroughly disturbed by the looting activity. Probably the looters had taken some original items. The remaining material must have been considered worthless and appears to have been scattered both in the two original cuts and over the floor (Table 2.4).

TABLE 2.4
Structure 5C-49: Time Spans

Time Span	Special Deposit	Comment
1		Period of abandonment and collapse and looting of special deposits.
2	PD. 181, PD. 182	Period of occupancy on Fl. 1 as modified by installation of special deposits, axial bench, and jamb blocks.
3		Period of occupancy on Fl. 1.
4		Period of occupancy on Fl. 2/3.
5		Period of primary construction; ca. 6,000 m^3 of masonry.

III

Structure 5D-77

Occupying the NE margin of the Lost World Plaza (Fig. 13a), Str. 5D-77 presents a striking spectacle. A single stretch of wall stands while all else has fallen. The odd thing is that the standing wall segment is almost, or perhaps completely, full height, and supports an unusually vertical half-vault unit. Despite the advanced state of collapse over most of the structure, depth of debris appears slight.

Loten and Lanza recorded 5D-77 in the summer of 1968 under the Tikal Standing Architectural Survey Program, a surface survey of standing architecture. This is an instance of a structure that technically qualifies as "standing," but hardly presents the degree of accessible detail needed for the architectural survey. Nevertheless, it is included here, partly because it provides a clear wall and vault section and it presents an intriguing challenge for reconstruction.

Maler (Tozzer 1911) either missed 5D-77 or deliberately ignored it. The Tozzer/Merwin map shows it as a standard "Tikal Temple," number 65, but no mention is made of it in the text (Tozzer 1911).

Frontal orientation of the structure is to the S. Cardinal orientation is weakly given by distorted rear wall faces as about 3° S of magnetic E (azimuth 93°).

Construction Stages

Lower Substructure, Building Platform, and Building Walls

LOWER SUBSTRUCTURE

Debris contours (Fig. 14b) and erosion at the wall base imply a lower substructure platform about 4.5 m high. It is tentatively reconstructed as only one terrace, but this merely reflects lack of data. The volume of masonry represented, assuming absence of any earlier structure, is approximately 1,200 m^3.

BUILDING PLATFORM

A hard plaster surface runs under exterior wall masonry (Fig. 15:4). This could be the top surface of a building platform component. The same surface appears at the interior and constitutes the primary room floor. It is hard, white, and smooth, about 4 cm thick on ballast graded from pebbles to cobbles. In other words, this is a well-made floor. Total thickness is unclear and no surface masonry is visible. For an estimated height of 0.50 m, total masonry volume is about 80 m^3.

BUILDING WALLS

If it is a valid assumption that no debris has been removed, the front wall (S) appears to have contained multiple doorway openings (Fig. 13b, 14a). Debris contours do not hint at any particular number. At section B-B', wall height is 2.73 m, and presumably this would apply over the entire building. Thickness at the wall foot is 1.46 m. The interior face is vertical and the exterior face has a slight positive batter (0.12/2.73, or 4%).

Wall-facing masonry, interior and exterior, employs large, roughly rectangular, horizontally bedded blocks (Table 3.1).

Course levels run unbroken through all visible surviving masonry and it is probable that levels run consistently around the building. The lower value of standard deviation (Table 3.1) for heights reflects coursing regularity. Exterior course levels correspond to interior levels. The work probably proceeded level by level over the whole building with interior faces carried up at the same time as exterior faces. Stretchers predominate over headers; the latter are readily identifiable and appear to be the same blocks simply laid with their length projecting into the core. Mortar joints are thick, spalls frequent, and relatively large. Interior facings are made of units slightly smaller than those on the exterior, but otherwise are very similar. Core masonry includes many stones identical to facing units, similarly bedded, with smaller rubble and aggregate filling in between.

A small exposure of face plaster remains at the interior vault spring. It is thick, gray, and on a white scratch coat. No exterior face plaster remains on exposed surfaces. Following masonry installation, face surfaces may have been roughly hammered to create a moderately good wall plane. It is likely, though, that the finish undulated somewhat.

Wall-top plaster is present at section B-B'. It is white, soft, and rather rough. It could not have endured exposure for very long before being covered by vault masonry.

Walls appear to define a single room approximately 29 m long by 3 m wide; this is a length-to-width ratio of 1:9.7. Two doorways open through the rear (N) wall. Their locations flanking the central axis do not suggest through-circulation. An indeterminate number of doorways may have extended across the front (S). About 26 m is available for front doorways, ample space for nine doorways of about 2 m each.

On the assumption that doorway openings amounted to about 40% of the front wall, and assuming rear wall thickness applies throughout, the total volume of wall masonry is 194 m^3.

Vaulting

One section of the N half-vault stands to a height of 3.5 m above the wall top (Fig. 14b, 15). From an outset spring, the soffit face rises almost vertically. With no soffit overhang, there is no problem of stability and no need for end-vault units; this rear half-vault can stand alone.

Relatively large room width (3 m) makes reconstructing the roof system problematic. The amount of debris seems inadequate for a similar half-vault unit on the S wall. Therefore, assuming that no debris has been removed, a roof is reconstructed half in thatch and half in masonry (Fig. 14b).

TABLE 3.1
Structure 5D-77: Face Dimensions of Wall-Facing Stretchers

Dimension	n	Mean (m)	Standard Deviation	Range (m)
Exterior Face Length	42	0.68	7.85	0.54–0.85
Exterior Face Height	42	0.20	1.42	0.17–0.23
Interior Face Length	33	0.43	17.21	0.26–0.75
Interior Face Height	33	0.20	2.75	0.14–0.29

Forced by the enigmatic nature of existing features, this hybrid roof system seems unlikely. If masonry vaulting had the special advantage of supporting sculptural treatment, one would expect this to be employed at the front rather than at the rear. Sculptural elaboration normally appears on frontal parts and more rarely on rear parts, although there are exceptions (5D-96). Perhaps the rear facade featured some kind of sculptural treatment.

Three levels of vault-beam sockets are visible in the surviving stretch of soffit face. Vertical intervals between socket holes imply that the vault stands very close to the original full height. Interestingly, beam sockets correspond to masonry-course levels. That is, the beams could have been placed as the masonry rose up rather than prior to masonry installation, as is more common. Perhaps these sockets do not represent falsework erected to establish soffit angles. If indeed thatching roofed the S half of the room, then a very different kind of timber construction would have been involved. The surviving sockets may be evidence of this.

The surviving half-vault stands 21 courses high. Soffit facers are horizontally bedded on the soffit face, and all appear to be stretchers. From the section (Fig. 15), many of the facing stones must be deep slabs. Wall and vault masonry appear similar in section, but face patterns differ; in the vault, headers are not evident, whereas they are clear in the wall. Therefore, it seems that special, more slablike masonry units were cut for the vault. Apart from this distinction, vault construction is very similar to wall construction (Table 3.2).

An irregular vault-back surface is clearly visible at the rear (Fig. 15:1). It is rough, undulating, and finished with mortar, that is to say, unplastered. It turned down onto medial molding corbels that have all fallen out. The interior soffit surface appears to have been finished with thick gray plaster on a white scratch coat. No paint remains.

Assuming no end-vault units and only one half-vault, the volume of vault masonry is 110 m^3.

Upper Zone

An upper zone appears to have existed only at the rear, if the reconstruction of Fig. 14b is accurate (also see Fig. 15). Its thickness could not have been more than about 2 cm and its finish is unknown. Modeled stucco on a mortar backing could have been installed in such a shallow layer. There is hardly any room for a masonry facing. The two rear doorways may hint at some significance attached to the N facade.

A rectangular opening runs through the vault mass about 1.36 m above spring level (Fig. 15:2). This appears to be a vent and presumably opened through the upper zone as well.

Thatching

Evidence for this final construction stage is mainly of the negative sort (Fig. 14b). That is, there is not enough debris to support reconstruction of vaulting on the S side of the room. Holes described above as vault-beam sockets may actually represent beams involved in a pole structure supporting thatched roofing.

Secondary Modifications

Three refloorings are visible at section B-B' (Fig. 15); the top two are mere skim coats. The first reflooring is a plaster topping on 6 cm of floor body.

TABLE 3.2
Structure 5D-77: Vault-Soffit Facing Stone Dimensions

Dimension	n	Mean (m)	Standard Deviation	Range (m)
Face Length	40	0.43	15.71	0.24–0.84
Face Height	40	0.16	1.97	0.13–0.20

All three turn up to primary wall masonry. Absence of wall plaster under these floor edges implies that the original wall finish had eroded by the time the secondary resurfacings were installed.

Architecture

With a width-to-length ratio of 1:6.1, Str. 5D-77 probably belongs in the "range-type" category of structures, although it has only one room. The ratio of substructure height to superstructure height, 1:1.6, also may support this assignment. Tentatively, 5D-77 may fit into a subcategory defined by multiple doorways, possibly as many as nine in the front facade. Its single room points to a subclassification. A third subcategory may be indicated by the presence of doorways in the rear facade. The roofing system, half thatch and half vault over the same room, may place the structure in a class of its own.

The fabric presents both early and late attributes. Those that appear early include a surface running under the wall that forms the primary room floor; roughly finished, undulating wall surfaces; thick gray plaster; and vault stones relatively unspecialized, neither toothed nor tapered. The late attributes include the plastered wall top; consistent coursing; and vault-back facing (Table 3.3).

TABLE 3.3
Structure 5D-77: Time Spans

Time Span	Units and Floors	Comment
1		Abandonment and collapse.
2	Three refloorings	Period of occupancy on secondary floor resurfacings.
3	Primary room floor	Period of occupancy as initially built.
4		Period of primary construction, approximately 1,600 m^3 of masonry.

IV

Structure 5D-84

Poor preservation almost excludes Str. 5D-84 from the survey of standing architecture. Only a small portion of exterior wall and a few bits of interior wall protrude above debris. These fragments suggest a layout for the building that may be reasonably accurate, so it has been included here.

Loten and Lanza completed the survey in 1966. The structure lies in the agglomerated series between the Lost World Plaza and the Plaza of the Seven Temples in the NW quadrant of the site epicenter (Fig. 16a).

The Tozzer/Merwin map (Tozzer 1911) shows 5D-84 as structure number 62, well N of structure 63 (our 5D-86). In fact, debris contours merge and there is no great space between the two. Not surprisingly, neither Tozzer nor Maler had anything to say about 5D-84.

Orientation is problematic in that debris appears to indicate stairs projecting to both E and W. The building plan (Fig. 16b), however, has two distinct parts and one of these probably is the principal front. As a guess, the structure probably faced to the W. A debris saddle implies presence of doorways above both E and W stairs. Circulation, then, may have proceeded through the building. Perhaps 5D-84 served as a formal link between the Lost World Plaza and Plaza of the Seven Temples.

Two short lengths of interior wall surface in the E room indicate an orientation of 3.5° E of magnetic N.

Construction Stages

Lower Substructure, Building Platform, and Building Walls

LOWER SUBSTRUCTURE

Total substructure height appears to be about 10 m (Fig. 17). Lower substructure height might be about 8 m if a building platform accounts for some of this. Two terraces of about 4 m are assumed for the lower component, but without any supporting evidence. The format illustrated in Fig. 16b is entirely conjectural.

If stairs were present on both E and W facades, they would make up a large part of the material needed for construction. If no earlier structure exists under 5D-84, the volume of material is roughly 2,000 m^3.

BUILDING PLATFORM

Two wall planes survive above debris on the N facade (Fig. 16b). The E plane lies about 4 cm N of the W plane. This indicates a building component of two parts. If there is a building platform, it should correspond to this configuration. In such cases at Tikal, parts formed by shifts in plan also present sectional shifts. If there are two parts to the building platform, one is probably higher than the other, but deep excavation is needed to establish this. Therefore, in Fig. 17, the top of the building platform appears as a broken line with no change in level. Its position corresponds to a small exposure of interior floor surface at the N end of the E room. Whether this is in fact the top surface of the building platform remains unclear.

No material definitely identifiable as part of a building platform is visible above debris. The volume of masonry required for the assumed building platform is roughly 200 m³.

BUILDING WALLS

Walls and also vaults are the only components of the structure that offer any extant elements for direct observation without excavation. Whether it was built as a distinct stage of construction is unclear in that the surface sustaining the walls lies deeply buried in debris.

A return face in the N facade indicates that the W part is not as wide as the E, and, from debris profiles, the W part appears to be shallower as well. An exterior W wall is shown, but its position is not known.

Wall-facing masonry employs subrectangular units, roughly shaped, irregularly coursed, and undifferentiated as headers and stretchers. Face dimensions range from 0.25 to 0.60 m in length. Average height is 2 cm. Average depth face-to-butt is 3 cm. Bedding joints are thick and stuffed with spalls. Interior and exterior facings are similar. Core masonry is not similar to facing masonry. The single extant portion of wall top is not plastered.

Part of an inset panel is visible in the E wall element of the N facade. For symmetry, a corresponding panel is assumed in the S facade.

A single medial corbel stone remains in place on the N facade at the corner between E and W building parts. It measures 1.25 by 1.25 by 0.22 m.

A hard, smooth plaster floor turns up to the interior wall face at the N end of the E room. No wall plaster remains on accessible surfaces. It is not clear if the floor is primary or secondary.

Assuming a wall height of 2.8 m results in a masonry volume of 125 m³.

Vaulting

Depth of debris implies presence of vaulting, but no specialized stones are visible. Absence of wall-top plaster indicates that workers installed walls and vaults with no formalized pause between these operations. That is, there appears to be no wall-top plaster.

Figure 17 provides a conventional vault profile not based on any firm data. The masonry volume represented is about 110 m³.

Upper Zones

The one extant medial corbel indicates presence of an upper-zone surface, but there may have been no real distinction between vault masonry and upper-zone material. The apparent upper zone may be coincident with the vault-back surface.

Roofcomb

The amount of debris seems sufficient for upper-zone and vault material. Therefore, a roofcomb is not assumed.

Relationship to Adjacent Stratigraphy

The architectural survey did not shed any light on stratigraphic relationships. Proyecto Nacional Tikal has provided this data while at the same time revealing a radically different architectural format (Laporte and Fialko 1995).

Architecture

Assumed presence of aligned E-W doorways, facilitating through-circulation, would characterize 5D-84 as a portal structure if, in fact, such doorways really are present. Debris profiles suggest aligned openings, but only with excavation can this be established. The structure seems oddly positioned for formal entry to either the Lost World Plaza or the Plaza of the Seven Temples.

Of the few accessible features, several indicate an early date of construction. These include absence of plastered wall tops; unspecialized vault stones; thick masonry joints with many spalls; subrectangular wall-facing stones roughly shaped and blocklike; and facing masonry not specialized as headers and stretchers.

It should be noted that the very different findings of Laporte and Fialko (1995) illustrate the problematic nature of surface survey in conditions of advanced collapse and deep debris (Table 4.1).

TABLE 4.1
Structure 5D-84: Time Spans

Time Span	Units and Floors	Comment
1		Period of abandonment and collapse.
2	Floor in E room?	Period of use as initially built: ca. 1,000 m^3 allowing for earlier construction (Laporte and Fialko 1995).

V

Structure 5D-86

On the E side of the Lost World Plaza, Str. 5D-86 faces W toward Str. 5C-54 (Fig. 18a). Forest cover gives this SW quadrant of the site a remote feeling, but in fact it is part of the Tikal epicenter, linked to the Great Plaza by continuous paved surfaces (Fig. 18b). The Tozzer/Merwin map notes Str. 5D-86 as number 63 but, probably due to advanced deterioration, neither Maler nor Tozzer gave it more than passing mention.

Loten and Lanza recorded 5D-86 in 1966. Its collapse is advanced (Fig. 19a,b, 20a,b). One vault fragment still stands at the N end of Rm. 3 (Fig. 20a, 21a,b) above debris that fills the rooms and conceals all substructure details. Directional orientation is problematic; side inset corners establish a line running 2.8° W of N magnetic (4° E of true N). With this as a baseline the structure may be said to face 4° S of true W.

Long after the Tikal Project, Proyecto Nacional Tikal discovered that 5D-86 is the sixth and final member of an architectural development (Laporte and Fialko 1995). Their mapping places 5D-86 and 5C-54 on a common central axis in a formation known as the E-Group Complex. If this arrangement really served for solar observations, the South Acropolis must have been either absent or much lower.

Construction Stages

Lower Substructure and Building Platform

LOWER SUBSTRUCTURE

Almost all substructure features are buried in collapse debris (Fig. 21a,b, 23). Figure 22 shows a conjectural plan arrangement. The 8 m height is divided arbitrarily into two terraces, although three might be equally probable. From building platform evidence, a rear axial outset is assumed—that it overrides both terraces (Fig. 23) is conjectural.

At the front, debris contours indicate a fully projecting stair. A hard, smooth plaster surface can be seen running under building platform material at the rear center (Fig. 23:1), and this surface should be the lower substructure top. A thickness of 2 cm of fine-grained hard plaster rests on core masonry, and there does not appear to be any floor ballast here. The small sample of visible core masonry is made up of horizontally bedded slabs in mortar no thicker than the joints of building wall facings. Core masonry units appear very similar to wall facing and core units (Fig. 21b). No facing masonry is visible and no paint can be seen, but since walls were painted red it seems likely that the substructure was similarly finished.

The volume of material needed, absent earlier construction, is 3,500 m³. The Proyecto Nacional Tikal section (Laporte and Fialko 1995:fig. 27) shows that earlier construction occupies more than half of this volume, perhaps 60%, so a rough estimate of lower substructure masonry is 2,000 m³.

BUILDING PLATFORM

The only visible outer face of this component is its top surface, a floor 0.12 m thick made up of 0.04 m of gray plaster topping, not particularly hard, on 0.08 m of pebble ballast in a dark mortar matrix (Fig. 23:1). Roughly shaped blocks horizontally bedded make up the core, at least in this exposure. Core masonry appears similar to wall masonry.

The three rooms step up from front to rear and, therefore, it is most likely that the building platform has three corresponding levels. Debris contours at the rear imply presence of a rear axial outset. A frontal stair is assumed, but debris is so deep here that no hint of it is visible. Side insets are assumed but are not reflected in debris profiles. Total masonry volume is 250 m³.

Walls

Prior to building construction, workers had completed the building platform and plastered over its top to provide the sustaining surface for the walls (Fig. 22–25a). Wall, vault, and upper-zone construction then proceeded with no distinct plastered pause-lines between them. At the front, medial molding stones pass through from exterior to interior (Fig. 21b), and this would amount to a pause of sorts between wall and vault/upper-zone work. At the N end of Rm. 2, however, medial molding corbels clearly do not extend all the way through (Fig. 25a). A leveling course is visible immediately under the medial molding corbels in this N side inset. At interior locations lacking medial moldings, there is no evident break between wall and vault features (Fig. 20a).

Wall surfaces are mainly visible on the exterior at the sides and rear (Fig. 19b). A few interior surfaces rise above debris filling the rooms (Fig. 19a, 21a). Wall construction conspicuously lacks core masonry (Fig. 21b). Butt surfaces of interior and exterior blocks abut at wall center, and interior and exterior faces are very similar. Masonry units are flat slabs horizontally bedded in courses that run only short distances. Mortar joints and beds range from 3 to 1 cm in thickness and are filled with large spalls, roughly 16 to the meter. All units are stretchers; there are, necessarily, no headers (Table 5.1).

High values of standard deviation for lengths indicate little standardization. Heights are more strictly controlled, although coursing is irregular. Dimensional variation suggests that the same source and stockpile were used for both interior and exterior face units. In fact, builders may have quarried stones for both interior and exterior indiscriminately.

At the N side inset, primary wall surface is finished with a single coat of thin, hard, dark gray plaster painted red (Fig. 25a:1, 5). Probably all exterior walls were painted red. Interiors retain no such traces but there are no similarly protected overhangs

TABLE 5.1
Structure 5D-86: Wall-Facing Stone Dimensions

Dimension	n	Mean (m)	Standard Deviation	Range (m)
Exterior Face Length	66	0.52	10.80	0.26–0.74
Exterior Face Height	66	0.17	2.41	0.13–0.24
Interior Face Length	21	0.46	13.30	0.24–0.73
Interior Face Height	21	0.18	4.04	0.12–0.25

where paint might remain. Extant faces are essentially vertical but very uneven and undulating.

Wall heights vary from 2.0 to 2.6 m as measured from estimated floor levels to vault springs. Thicknesses are more constant at 0.90 m. The thickness-to-height ratio at the rear axial outset is 1:2.9. That is, this wall height is nearly three times its thickness.

Three inset panels survive above in standing walls (Fig. 19a, 22, 24, 26a). The total number prior to partial collapse is probably five. The three extant panels are all different. In the N facade (Fig. 19b, 24:inset panel [I.P.] 1), the jamb channels extend right through the wall. On the rear axial outset (I.P. 3), the channels extend only part way through and to different depths (Table 5.2). On the S facade rear facet (I.P. 4), one channel runs through, the other does not, and all appear primary. All jamb surfaces are plastered.

The N side inset wall has a primary opening into Rm. 1 (Fig. 25a:7). It is located 0.50 m below wall-top level, well above normal eye-level. Probably it was installed as a vent. Jamb and sill surfaces are plastered. Stone slabs span the opening. Variation in the surviving panels makes it impossible to reconstruct those fallen with any confidence beyond the assumption that the two missing ones occupy symmetrical locations.

Where walls are not fallen or debris covered, 11 holes can be seen, 10 at exterior surfaces and 1 in Rm. 2 (Fig. 24). Some are at the wall foot, others about 2.5 m higher and vertically aligned. The holes are higher than they are wide, probably because wall stones were not cut to fit around the timbers. Gaps above the timbers would have been filled with mortar and small aggregate that has now fallen out. In general, it appears that masonry units were not shaped to fit in specific locations, but rather were accepted on the job site as they were shaped at the quarry.

All doorways are either collapsed or debris covered. Their locations can be seen in debris contours. No lintels survive. A representative doorway width, 2.0 m, estimated from debris profiles, is applied arbitrarily to all doorways.

ROOMS

The three rooms, arranged in tandem, vary greatly in size. The front room, already the largest, is further amplified by a recess or setback in the center part of the rear wall (Fig. 24). The middle room is barely half as wide and only two-thirds as long. The rear room is almost as wide as the front room but much shorter. Although a rear axial niche might be expected in Rm. 3, the depth of jamb channels in the rear inset panel seems to preclude this and no evidence of a niche is visible.

The three rooms add up to a total area of 212 m² within a gross building area of 423 m². The ratio of room area to gross area is almost exactly 1:2. Total volume of wall masonry is 150 m³.

Vaulting

Vaults at 1.5 m are all similar in height, but because of differing room widths their profiles change dramatically (Fig. 23). Even though only partially accessible, vault springs present different conditions. Some are outset normally, others hardly at all. Spring heights vary as well, even within rooms. The only

TABLE 5.2
Structure 5D-86: Inset Panel Dimensions

Inset Panel Number	Width (m)	Height (m)	Sill Height (m)*	Channel Depth (m)	Comment
1	1.10	0.65	1.00	na	Through wall.
3	2.43	1.00	0.73	0.20/0.40	
4	1.15	?	?	0.20/na	One channel runs through.

* Above wall foot

TABLE 5.3
Structure 5D-86: Face Dimensions of Vault-Soffit Stones

Dimension	n	Mean (m)	Standard Deviation	Range (m)
Half-Vault Face Length	11	0.33	9.34	0.23–0.57
Half-Vault Face Height	11	0.18	5.53	0.11–0.33
End-Vault Face Length	6	0.32	8.57	0.25–0.45
End-Vault Face Height	6	0.11	1.00	0.10–0.12

measurable soffit profiles are in Rm. 2 (Fig. 20a, 25a). Soffit stones are not specialized nor dressed to a consistent profile. All plastering was done after capstones had been installed. Soffits vary from six to eight or more courses. The spring course in Rm. 1 projects through from interior to exterior on the W face but not on the N face. Capstones are similar in form to soffit stones, ca. 0.10 m thick by 0.40 m wide and 0.70 m long. They were not preplastered. Core masonry is not accessible and probably vaults were built like walls, with the same stones used in core and soffit facing. The one end-vault condition observable (Fig. 25a) is faced with smaller stones (Table 5.3).

Values of standard deviation, despite small sample size, indicate somewhat greater dimensional uniformity than in wall construction. For vault construction, stones slightly smaller than wall stones and more similar to each other, were either selected from the common stockpile or specially quarried. Their shapes are not unlike wall stones. Mortar joints are similar to those of the walls, thick and filled with spalls. A single plaster coat is applied directly onto the soffit facers and no post-dressing had been applied to the soffit face.

A single pair of socket holes near the N end of Rm. 2 reveals the presence of vault beams. The one beam indicated appears to have been about 0.10 m in diameter, probably unworked. No beam pattern could be discerned without excavation.

Upper Zones

Workers probably did not fully complete vault construction before installing the upper zones; both seem to have been part of the same operation. Three upper-zone levels can be seen, stepping up from front to rear and corresponding with some vault-spring levels. At the front of the building, there are medial moldings and superior moldings but no corner or "hip" moldings. The *tablero* format is not present (Fig. 25a). At the N side inset, a similar condition prevails. The rear upper zone has no moldings (Fig. 23).

Upper-zone masonry closely resembles wall and vault masonry. The medial corbels that support the upper-zone outset and form front and side inset moldings are the largest stones visible in extant fabric not hidden by debris. A typical example is 0.40 by 0.40 by 1.00 m. The length dimension extends through the front wall and into the core at the rear. The corner medial corbel visible in Fig. 19b measures 1.05 by 0.87 by 0.22 m thick. Traces of red paint remain on the undersurface of medial corbels.

The N side inset retains a sculptural motif executed in thick stucco and retaining traces of red paint (Fig. 19b, 25b, 26a,b). Two scrolls and a central plaque appear to be basal elements of a lost sculptural feature. Iconographically, this motif is related to the sky symbolism and is of a type found in early sculptural programs, reaching back into the Late Preclassic period (400 BC–250 AD) (Taube 1996:91). There are no projecting armature stones above the surviving fragment. Evidently modeling was entirely in stucco and did not develop relief of more than about 5 cm. Mortar and small aggregate covering the stucco feature can be seen at the right edge in Fig. 26b. Apparently, the sculptural feature had been secondarily concealed.

Upper-zone height, in front and rear facets, compares to wall height in the ratio of 1:1.6; walls are more than half again as high as the upper zones.

A small fragment of roof surface remains above upper-zone material at the N end of Rm. 2 (Fig. 25a). It is 3 cm thick and was placed directly on top of vault capstones. The roof does not retain paint traces and shows no sign of weathering. It does indicate completion of the building stage of construction.

There is no masonry volume assignable to the upper zones. Essentially, upper-zone surfaces are vault-back surfaces.

Roofcomb

The small remnant of material overlying the roof surface at the N end of Rm. 2 (Fig. 25a) presumably represents a roof structure of some kind. Assumed is a substantial roofcomb on the basis of the quantity of debris in and around the building and over the substructure. A representative volume of roofcomb masonry, 75 m^3, allows for the possible presence of chambers.

Secondary Modifications

As noted above, a layer of mortar and aggregate overlies the sculptural feature in the N upper-zone side inset (Fig. 25a). This material probably would have filled the area between the medial molding and the superior molding to form a plain profile like that of the rear faces. Concealment of the sculptural feature may have reflected ideological issues.

Below this modified upper-zone element a secondary coat of plaster was applied over the primary plaster. It is 2 cm thick, that is, thicker than primary plaster and lighter gray in color. No traces of paint survive. The application appears to have been limited to the side inset face. If unpainted between red elements in front and rear, the effect would have been to further emphasize the separation between front and rear parts that the side inset establishes. This would reinforce perception of the building as a fabric made up of two distinct entities.

Relationship to Adjacent Stratigraphy

The architectural survey could not establish any relationship to adjacent features without engaging in excavation beyond the scope of the surface survey. Proyecto Nacional Tikal has subsequently determined these relationships (Laporte and Fialko 1995).

Architecture

Structure 5D-86 represents an architectural category defined by the presence of side insets; rear axial outsets; roofcomb; three rooms in tandem stepping up from front to rear; and three frontal doorways. A subcategory is based on the presence of side insets in the building platform. Substructure height, which could prescribe a subcategory, is problematic in this case due to the presence of earlier construction influencing height. Red paint may be another factor bearing on classification.

Relatively great lateral expansion of the front part beyond the rear part suggests an early date of construction. Other attributes supporting this include absence of wall-top plaster; absence of masonry post-dressing; a floor running under building walls; thick stucco modeling not on a stone armature; capstones not preplastered; unspecialized vault-soffit stones; very weak discontinuous coursing of wall masonry; relatively thin walls; and relatively low upper zones in relation to wall height (Table 5.4).

TABLE 5.4
Structure 5D-86: Time Spans

Time Span	Comment
1	Period of abandonment and collapse.
2	Period of occupancy as modified by concealment of sculptural motif and replastering of side inset.
3	Period of occupancy as initially built.
4	Period of construction: roughly 6,000 m^3 of masonry.

VI

Structure 5D-87

The great majority of architectural survey structures–those not included in other operations, yet presenting standing features—are freestanding entities. Structure 5D-87 is the exception. It appears in the linear agglutination of Str. 5D-82 through 89 (Fig. 27a). These fabrics separate the so-called Lost World Plaza, which they face, from the Plaza of the Seven Temples in the SW quadrant of the site center.

Structure 5D-87 stands near the center of the Plaza of the Seven Temples, onto which it turns its back. It lies distinctly S of the centerline of Str. 5C-54, which it faces (W). Its front features are fallen and its sides and rear stand clear of debris. Lower substructure features are obscured beneath collapse debris and the upper part of the roofcomb has fallen.

The best orientation available is the line defined by the N and S rear building corners that bears 2° W of magnetic N. This corresponds to 4°, 45' E of true N (TR. 11).

Loten did the recording in 1966 with the assistance of Lanza. According to the terms of reference for the architectural survey, underbrush clearing was minimal and only a few features very close to the surface were clarified by limited excavation.

Sustaining Surface

Subsequent to the Tikal Project, the Proyecto Nacional Tikal showed that 5D-87 had been erected in front of and above a five-doorway, range-type structure facing E to the Plaza of the Seven Temples (Laporte and Fialko 1995:fig. 54). A part of the upper zone of this buried structure is now exposed.

Construction Stages

Lower Substructure, Building Platform, and Building Walls

LOWER SUBSTRUCTURE

The form of this feature is not known (Fig. 28, 29). Its height is approximately 9 m but, as we now know, it overlies earlier construction. Its existence as a distinct construction stage, completed before work began on the building platform, is merely assumed.

Figure 28 shows a highly conjectural arrangement except for the stair, which seems indicated by contour profiles. Rounded corners are based on building platform attributes (discussed below). The volume implied in Fig. 28 is roughly 5,000 m³. By subtracting earlier construction, the amount of masonry needed for this final version of 5D-87 might be as little as 700 m³. Most of this, 500 m³, forms the stair.

BUILDING PLATFORM

There are three distinct parts to the building platform (Fig. 28, 30, 31a–c). The front part is 1.3 m high, the middle is 1.5 m high, and the rear part is 1.75 m high. A stair of perhaps four risers is assumed at the front. A side inset separates front and rear parts. A small excavation at the NW front corner revealed a rounding of roughly 0.30 m in radius. The rounding is a compound curve perhaps closer to a parabola than a circle. Probably the curve was cut by eye without any specific geometry in mind. It begins with a relatively large radius that decreases progressively toward the corner. Similar rounding is assumed for all substructure corners.

The same small excavation exposed an apron molding of the three-part type (Fig. 31a). The upper part, or "apron," amounts to 60% of total height and the middle, or "subapron," to 18%. Absence of an apron molding on the rear axial outset is assumed.

Workers employed about 174 m³ of masonry for the building platform.

BUILDING WALLS

Construction staging is confused here by contradictory evidence (Fig. 32–34). Two different conditions appear at the N and S side insets (Fig. 32). The N inset wall stands on a hard plaster surface stained by burning. The S inset wall stands on a rough mortar surface. On the basis of the S condition, building platform and building walls formed parts of one construction stage. The N condition implies a significant pause and some kind of activity between the building platform and the walls.

The ratio of room area to gross building area is 1:14. As indicated in Fig. 34, building walls vary greatly in thickness. Front walls are under debris, but the SW corner indicates a thickness of about 1 m. The spine wall, between Rm. 1 and Rm. 2, is 1.45 m thick. At the rear axial outset, the rear wall is 2.9 m thick. The dimension from the S end wall of Rm. 2 to the rear exterior wall surface is 3.85 m. Front walls are 2.72 m high, the spine wall is 3 m high, and the rear wall is 2.40 m high. All wall surfaces are vertical. Wall tops are finished with hard, smooth plaster and lintel beds are similar.

Eleven scaffolding holes are visible across exterior surfaces (Fig. 30, 34) at upper levels (that is, above debris). In two cases, lower vertically aligned holes show that these really are for scaffolding (Fig. 34).

Only one doorway opening, Dr. 2, is measurable near the debris surface (Fig. 30, 33, 34) and is 1.77 m wide.

Exterior wall-facing stones are of veneer type set in continuous courses with stretchers predominating. Headers are easily recognizable and sporadically distributed. Stretcher face lengths vary from 0.43 to 0.67 m; mean value is 0.58 m; standard deviation is 4.69. This is a relatively low sigma value indicating a high level of dimensional control and standardization. Representative thickness for stretchers is 0.16 m with butt surfaces smooth and flat. Headers appear to have the same dimensions as stretchers, simply set with length projecting into the wall core. Joints and beds are thin at the surface and spalls are rare. Face surfaces of exterior walls have been shaved to a smooth plane following installation of masonry units. Interior facings are plaster covered, smooth and regular, similar to exteriors. Both interior and exterior surfaces have a single coat of white plaster, 1 cm thick, hard, and smooth. There are no visible traces of paint.

Exterior wall surfaces include five inset panels, all very similar in form (Fig. 30, 31c, 34). They have vertical jamb-channels averaging 0.10 m wide by 0.09 to 0.13 m deep. The inset panel on the rear axial outset is wider than the others (2.10 m) and slightly higher (0.59 m). Other panels vary from 1.03 to 1.10 m in width by 0.55 m in height.

Total volume of masonry in walls is 190 m³.

Vaulting

To begin the next construction stage, workers installed wood lintels on previously prepared, plastered beds (Fig. 29, 32, 33). No evidence remains for lintels over exterior front doorways. Mortar casts at Dr. 2 indicate a lintel of five squared beams; representative dimensions are 0.16 m deep by 0.26 m wide. For structural efficiency, the maximum dimension should be in the vertical rather than the horizontal, but evidently the builders were not worried about this. A thin fillet of mortar extends down between each beam to the undersurface. This may mean that the lintel was plastered on its underside.

With lintels in place, supra-lintel masonry could be placed up to wall-top level, the first course of vault stones placed, setting the vault-springs. On either side of Dr. 2, wooden dowels were set in the mortar between these vault-spring stones. They are indicated by two rod-row holes 0.02 and 0.03 m in diameter by 0.21 and 0.31 m deep (Fig. 32:7). They angle upward and taper to a point. No others are visible.

A timber scaffolding, or falsework, was installed within Rm. 2, and probably also within Rm. 1, as

TABLE 6.1
Structure 5D-87: Vault-Beam Sockets in Room 2

Beam Number	Diameter (m)	Depth (m)	Level	Comment
1	0.11	1.15	Top	
2	0.12	0.77	Bottom	On wall top.
3	0.12	na	Middle	Extends through vault core.
4	0.07	0.42	Bottom	On wall top.
5	0.11	?	?	On wall top, part extant.
6	0.08	0.77	Top	
7	0.12	na	Middle	Extends through vault core.
8	0.15	na	Bottom	On wall top, extends through vault core.

preparation for vaulting. Vault-beam sockets provide the evidence for this. They do not coincide with course levels, except for the bottom row, set at wall-top level. Beams are arranged in a five-beam pattern except for one extra member, Bm. 4 (Fig. 32; Table 6.1).

Vault details can be seen in Rm. 2, while very little Rm. 1 vaulting remains, at least above debris. In Rm. 2, the spring level is 0.30 m higher than in Rm. 1. Soffits in Rm. 2 are four and five courses high, all headers, rectangular on the face, with maximum dimension in the vertical. Course heights vary (Table 6.2); mortar joints are thin and spalls infrequent.

Beam 5, the only one surviving, is an unmodified logwood unit, perhaps installed complete with bark. Presumably the others were similar.

In section, soffit stones taper sharply from face to butt. Face surfaces have been dressed to a smooth, straight-line profile after masonry installation.

The vault core between Rm. 1 and 2 consists of small aggregate (up to 0.10 m) in gray-brown, tight adhesive mortar. The collapse face above Dr. 2 (Fig. 33) resembles a vault-back but has no finished surface. Construction appears to have proceeded from the rear toward the front and involves 110 m³ of masonry.

Soffit plaster was applied while the gap between half-vaults was still open and preplastered capstones were then installed to close the gap. This would have been done after removal of timber scaffolding.

Upper Zones

There are two distinct upper-zone formats: a front pattern and a rear pattern. They are separated by the side inset. This element has a medial molding and an upper molding and then rises to engage with the roofcomb (Fig. 27b).

TABLE 6.2
Structure 5D-87: Face Dimensions of Vault-Soffit Headers

Unit Type	Dimension	n	Mean (m)	Standard Deviation	Range
Half-Vault	Face Length	34	0.27	3.17	0.20–0.33
Half-Vault	Face Height	34	0.30	2.68	0.20–0.35
End-Vault	Face Length	10	0.26	2.91	0.20–0.31
End-Vault	Face Height	10	0.30	1.69	0.28–0.33

Medial molding fragments survive at N and S sides adjacent to the side inset. From these remnants the framed, or *tablero* format illustrated in Fig. 27b and 30 can be inferred. No sculptural fragments are visible, but the surviving bits are in places not usually elaborated sculpturally. The front facade probably did include sculptural treatment, inferred from upper-zone moldings seen in Fig. 27b.

Fragmentary remains of hip moldings can be seen at the side insets (Fig. 27b). These confirm the *tablero* format. Further, they suggest that ancient Maya designers wanted the exterior front part of the building to be perceived as a complete whole. Moldings on the return face within the side inset and side insets in the building platform show this intention.

The rear upper zone, by contrast, has no moldings. A sculpture fragment survives at the center of the rear axial outset (Fig. 31b). This is probably part of a localized central rear motif. All the rest of it has fallen and its dimensions are not clear. The surviving single masonry unit is carved and incised and coated with thick plaster that replicates the details set out in the stone. No paint remains.

The roof of the building is a hard, plastered, horizontal surface visible above the double-vault mass between Rm. 1 and 2 (Fig. 33). At the rear, where upper-zone masonry has fallen, the roof surface does not appear. The plastered roof surface may not extend over the whole roof area. There is no evident subroof surface.

Volume of masonry employed for upper zone and roof construction is about 30 m^3.

Roofcomb

Extant roofcomb masonry exists to about 3 m above roof level. A plastered, smoothly finished vault-soffit face can be seen where material has fallen away at the S side. This indicates presence of at least one roofcomb chamber in the lower roofcomb level (Fig. 33). Depth of debris around the structure and the extreme rear wall thickness implies presence of an upper level. The roofcomb illustrated in Fig. 33 is conjectural in terms of height (8 m), but factual with respect to sculptural treatment. A sculpture fragment survives at the central base and appears to be a mask element with carved stones that are plaster covered (Fig. 31b). No paint remains. Facing stones at the roofcomb rear resemble those of the building exterior walls.

The masonry volume in the roofcomb might total about 200 m^3, an estimate made without knowing the number and size of chambers.

Secondary Modifications

No modifications are visible in accessible features.

Other Features

Signs of burning can be seen on the top surface of the building platform at the N side inset. A hole in the S side inset may be a scaffolding hole enlarged by animals, probably birds (Fig. 32:3).

Relationship to Adjacent Stratigraphy

Investigation of this subject is beyond the scope of the surface survey. Work of the Proyecto Nacional Tikal long after the Tikal Project shows that 5D-87 was built on top of earlier construction (Laporte and Fialko 1995).

Architecture

Structure 5D-87 fits into an architectural category defined by the presence of three front doorways, side insets, rear axial outset, and roofcomb. It belongs in a subset of this class with two rather than three rooms or one room. The exterior of these structures appears as two entities placed one in front of the other. Normally the front part has sculptural treatment while the rear does not. Exceptionally, in this case, the rear upper zone has sculptural treatment. Usually this appears only on the roofcomb. These structures are normally referred to as "temples." They constitute an architectural type that could be called the "Tikal Temple" (Loten 2006).

Exterior wall-facing stones of veneer type are diagnostic of relatively late construction. The same can be said for the practice of plastering the wall-top and lintel beds. Vault-soffit facing stones, too, are of late type, tapered, toothed, and not set up as corbels, except for the spring course. Preplastered capstones present another "late" feature together with post-dressing of masonry and thin, white plaster. Relative shallowness of side insets is another "late" attribute. These properties indicate clearly that 5D-

87 was built toward the end of the Classic period (Table 6.3).

From this perspective, it is remarkable that several Early Classic features are also present. These include the triple doorway facade, inset panels, the particular type of apron molding on the building platform, side insets in the building platform, and rounded substructure corners. At a late date of construction, these features must have been conscious archaisms. Perhaps some aspect of the institution housed by 5D-87 had strong links to Early Classic times.

TABLE 6.3
Structure 5D-87: Time Spans

Time Span	Comment
1	Abandonment and collapse.
2	Period of occupancy as originally built.
3	Construction over earlier fabric; approximately 1,300 m^3 of masonry.

VII

Structure 6D-1

At the outer edge of the SW quadrant of the site, the epicentral Str. 6D-1 faces W toward a set of six fully collapsed structures (Fig. 35a). These seven structures form a "T"-shaped grouping that occupies the center of a plaza projecting S from the sprawling epicentral complex.

Building walls stand above debris entirely obscuring the substructure. The vault has fallen almost completely. The structure clearly faces toward the W, but cardinal orientation is not measurable with much precision. The line generated by corners of the rear axial outset extends 1° W of magnetic N. The angle of the S face and rear part is 5.7° N of E. The true orientation may depart from both of these bearings.

No earlier investigations noted this structure.

Construction Stages

Lower Substructure Platform, Building Platform, and Building Walls

LOWER SUBSTRUCTURE PLATFORM

The lower substructure platform (Fig. 36) lies entirely beneath debris. Its top surface, the only part accessible without excavation, appears below the rear axial outset. A white plaster floor-like topping, 0.30 m thick, not particularly hard or smooth, overlies a graded ballast layer 0.20 m thick. This is a slightly rough but well-made surface. Core masonry appears to include some quite large units, and no facing masonry is accessible.

In the absence of data indicating otherwise, the top surface is projected from the rear front at the same level. The height is about 3 m above the estimated plaza level. Workers quarried and placed about 250 m³ of masonry for this component.

BUILDING PLATFORM

Workers installed the building platform and walls, two visually distinct parts, in the same construction stage. Therefore, they are classed as substages.

The only visible part of the building platform (Fig. 36) is at the rear axial outset. Here an apron profile has the subapron set very low, with no basal molding. The ratio of subapron height to apron height is 0.30:1.2, or 1:4. Batter is slight, 0.08 in 1.20 m, or 1:15 (note: a batter of 45° would be equivalent to a ratio of 1:1). A 1:15 ratio equates to an angle of 5°.

Presumably the building platform follows the lines of the building walls though this cannot be verified without excavation. In Fig. 35b, separate front and rear parts are shown conjecturally. The top surface, at the rear, is a rough mortar layer, not a plastered surface as would be the case if the building platform had been completed prior to work on the walls.

Facing masonry strongly resembles that of the walls of the building, described below.

As with the lower substructure platform, a single height, 1.4 m, is assumed for both front and rear parts. This assumption runs counter to normal practice at Tikal, but with only one room there is no opportunity for a level change unless the sustaining surface at the rear wall is higher than the room floor. The volume of masonry required is about 50 m³. The plan configuration illustrated in Fig. 35b is conjectural in all parts other than the rear axial outset.

BUILDING WALLS

Most of the rear wall and part of the S sidewall stand to full height, but only exterior surfaces are accessible without excavation (Fig. 35b, 36). An inset corner is clearly visible in the S facade. Its N counterpart is assumed. The side inset, as in many other Tikal structures, appears to divide the building into two parts externally, with the front part projecting laterally beyond the line of the rear part. From the outside one would expect at least two rooms, but there is only one room. Exterior form apparently follows an architectural convention that originated centuries earlier in buildings with two or three rooms arranged in tandem. Eventually this exterior format must have developed a value, and perhaps a symbolism, which was not dependent on, or linked to, the number of rooms.

Wall-facing stones are rectangular veneer units (ashlar), well cut and shaped, about 0.16 m thick. Coursing runs consistently through visible wall faces with headers and stretchers frequent but in no consistent pattern. Stonecutters maintained highly standardized dimensions (Table 7.1).

Mortar joints are thin and spalls are absent. Workers dressed face surfaces to a smooth wall plane after the masonry had been installed. The exterior rear outset face is vertical. No trace of plaster or paint remains on visible surfaces.

Interior wall facings have fallen at the one point where they might have been accessible with only very minor excavation (Fig. 36). Remaining in place are core units that must have been immediately behind the facing stones. From this, it appears interior facings resemble exterior facings.

At the rear axial outset, wall thickness is 2.16 m (allowing for fallen interior facings). Since the outset projects about 0.15 m, the rear wall thickness is probably almost exactly 2 m. Its height is 2.54 m. The thickness-to-height ratio is 1:1.27, that is, relatively thick. Side and front wall thicknesses, as shown in Fig. 35b, are conjectural but probably thinner. From debris profiles, and from the modest dimensions of the building, there appears to be a single front doorway.

Judging from the one accessible (SE) corner, the geometry of the building is distinctly skewed. This SE corner measures 97°. Broken-line portions of the plan (Fig. 35b) attempt to resolve this departure from strict rectangularity, but do so hypothetically.

Two inset panels are visible in standing walls. A third is assumed on the basis of symmetry. A wall-top surface is assumed, but the survey did not manage to access and record its location. The conjectural plan implies a wall masonry volume of about 65 m³.

Vaulting

A single soffit facing stone remains, perhaps a little displaced (Fig. 36). All others have fallen. The one remaining stone has top and bottom surfaces nearly parallel, and sides tapering to a narrow butt. The face is almost square (0.30 m).

The base level of vault-back facing remains immediately behind the medial corbel stone at the rear axial outset. The vault-back face is formed by small stones horizontally bedded, not dressed on face sur-

TABLE 7.1
Structure 6D-1: Face Dimensions of Exterior Wall Stretchers

Dimension	n	Mean (m)	Standard Deviation	Range (m)
Face Length	55	0.61	3.49	0.53–0.69
Face Height	55	0.31	1.08	0.29–0.34

faces. There is no sign of plaster. The medial corbel stone tapers to a narrow butt.

On the assumption that the one remaining vault-soffit facing stone is near the mid-height of the vault, the volume of masonry in the vault is about 25 m³.

Roof and Upper Zones

All that remains of the roof and upper zones is a short run of medial corbels in the N facade. Because of the plan arrangement, it seems likely that upper zones would be in two parts, the front part wider and lower than the rear part. This is indicated in Fig. 36, but is entirely suppositional. Equally conjectural is the notion that only the front part would have medial and superior moldings. An estimated masonry volume of 30 m³ accounts for upper zone and roof elements.

Roofcomb

The quantity of debris suggests the possible existence of a roofcomb. Figure 36 does not indicate a roofcomb, nor is there any obvious basis for an estimate of masonry volume.

Architecture

Side insets and rear axial outset place Str. 6D-1 in a category with many other Tikal structures displaying these features. Inset panels may define a subcategory. The modest size of the structure and its single room place it in a second subcategory.

Attributes that appear "late" include wall thickness; absence of a floor surface running under the walls; thin veneer facings; standardized facing-stone dimensions; specialized vault-soffit stone(s); the presence of a vault-back facing; and the very low subapron on the building platform.

A single "early" attribute contrasts with the above "late" features. This is the presence of inset panels in the building walls. From the preponderance of "late" attributes, a "late" date of construction seems indicated. Inset panels, then, may represent some kind of reference to much earlier work (Table 7.2).

TABLE 7.2
Structure 6D-1: Time Spans

Time Span	Comment
1	Period of abandonment and collapse.
2	Period of use as originally built.
3	Period of construction: approximately 420 m³ of masonry.

VIII

Conclusions

Four of the six examples of standing architecture described in this volume are either Middle Classic or Early Classic in date and two are clearly Late Classic. The earlier structures are 5C-49, 5D-77, 5D-84, and 5D-86; the later ones are 5D-87 and 6D-1. In the absence of stratigraphic controls, inscriptions, and ^{14}C dating, the above assessments reflect architectural characteristics of superstructures—substructure details were not accessible without excavation.

Architectural diagnostics of construction earlier than Late Classic at Tikal include masonry types, plan features, vaulting, and stucco work. In the four "early" structures, facing stones are relatively large blocks, roughly squared, sometimes called "cushion-shaped." Structures standing on the South Acropolis summit display this kind of masonry, not found in securely dated Early Classic or Late Classic contexts. Middle Classic is, therefore, a tentative dating assignment.

Structures 5C-49 and 5D-86 display "thin-wall" building construction. By itself, this attribute is most closely associated with Early Classic construction beneath and on the summit of the North Acropolis, and on the South Acropolis. Coupled with cushion-shaped wall-facing stones, "thin-wall" buildings are likely to be Middle Classic in date.

Surviving vault-soffit stones in 5C-49 and 5D-86 are not as highly specialized as we see in typical Late Classic work nor are they the flat rough slabs of Early Classic construction. Soffit faces are somewhat irregular, not smoothly dressed to precise profiles as is typical of Late Classic finishes at Tikal. This is an attribute of early construction, but these are not Early Classic Tikal vaults. Again, Middle Classic seems to emerge by default as the most likely dating assignment.

Structure 5D-77 is so bizarre that normative patterns hardly apply. Masonry of the cushion-block form may indicate a Middle Classic date though such an unusual construction, part vaulted and part thatched, throws any assignment into doubt.

On 5D-86 we see thick, dark gray, modeled stucco. This kind of relief sculpture appears on Early Classic buildings at Tikal on the North Acropolis summit and in earlier work overlaid by the summit complex.

Both 5D-87 and 6D-1 show typical Late Classic veneer masonry, smoothly dressed for thin plaster. The 5D-87 building is of the thick-wall type seen at Tikal only in Late Classic buildings. By itself this seems to be a reliable Late Classic diagnostic. There are complications, however. On exterior walls of both buildings we see inset panels. These are features that look like images of windows and may be elements of a "house" metaphor. They are also found in Early Classic work on the North Acropolis and so, by themselves, would be taken as indicators of Early Classic construction. Here they must be seen as intentional anachronisms or revivalist features.

It may be that in the SW quadrant builders and designers were less reluctant to discard centuries-old architecture features. On Str. 5D-86, for example, inset panels are not out of place, but on 5D-87 and 6D-1, much later constructions, these features seem like intentional anachronisms.

Five of the six examples of standing architecture described in this volume belong to a morphological type that probably can be described by the term "temple." Only 5D-77 diverges, apparently having multiple doorways, or perhaps an entirely open front, leading to a single room that may have been roofed by pole and thatch set up against a masonry rear wall–a unique arrangement within the set of structures investigated.

The other five show an essentially vertical format with rear axial outsets and, in the case of 5D-87, a towering roofcomb. Structure 5C-49 has a stubby roof structure, hardly a roofcomb, but its substructure is so high that "temple" classification seems appropriate. Rear axial outsets appear on all the Great Temples at Tikal and on the structures at the summit of the North Acropolis. They seem to be reliable temple diagnostics.

No temple definition has ever been widely accepted for Mesoamerican architecture, although the term itself is very widely employed. In TR. 23C, a functional definition is proposed based on the supposition that some structures were built in the expectation that non-human forces would occupy these fabrics during times of ceremonial performance. The rational behind this is that authorities of a city like Tikal would have wanted non-human forces to be present as witnesses to the rituals so that they would respond with positive support for Tikal enterprises. Caches, burials, signs of burning, and architectural features such as rear axial outsets, high pyramidal substructures, display setups such as prominent stairs, and associated stelae and altars, may provide evidence in support of such a definition.

Structure 6D-1 qualifies as a temple according to the definition offered above. It must be the smallest Tikal temple on record, and can hardly be described as "vertical." It does have the rear axial outset and also inset panels, features common to many other Tikal structures that would probably be called temples by any definition. Masonry characteristics, such as veneer facings, appear "late," when technical skills in construction were probably at their peak. Still, the layout is noticeably skewed. One might think that accurate right-angle corners would be easier to accomplish on a small structure than on a large one. Yet many much larger, more or less contemporary works at Tikal are much more regular.

It may be that square corners were only one of several factors directing layout. There may have been other considerations affecting the direction of E-W lines on the one hand and N-S lines on the other hand. Whatever targets were employed to determine base lines might have dictated corners that were not quite square. Great Temple III raises this same issue. The sun could have determined E-W lines, but there is no obvious basis for N-S ones. If these latter were meant to be perpendicular to the E-W lines, the corner would likely be closer to ninety degrees and not so obviously parallel at obtuse and acute angles.

The location chosen for Str. 6D-1, on a platform extending S, like a small annex to the epicenter, suggests a marginal status. Perhaps the builders did not have access to the full range of epicenter resources, and perhaps the builders and users did not even live in the epicenter.

References

Laporte, Juan Pedro, and Vilma Fialko
1995   Un reencuentro con Mundo Perdido, Tikal, Guatemala. *Ancient Mesoamerica* 6(1):41–94.

Loten, H. Stanley
2006   A Distinctive Architectural Format: The Lamanai Temple. In *Reconstructing the Past: Studies in Mesoamerican and Central American Prehistory*, edited by D.M. Pendergast and A.P. Andrews, pp. 89–106. BAR International Series 1529. Oxford: British Archaeological Reports.

Maler, Teobert
1911   *Explorations in the Department of Peten, Guatemala.* Memoirs of the Peabody Museum of Archaeology and Ethnology vol. 5 no. 1. Cambridge, MA: Peabody Museum of Archaeology and Ethnology, Harvard University.

Taube, Karl
1996   The Rainmakers: The Olmec and their Contribution to Mesoamerican Belief and Ritual. In *The Olmec World: Ritual and Kingship,* edited by Michael D. Coe, pp. 83–103. Princeton and New York: The Art Museum, Princeton University and Harry Abrams.

Tozzer, Alfred M.
1911   *Preliminary Study of the Ruins of Tikal, Guatemala.* Memoirs of the Peabody Museum of Archaeology and Ethnology vol. 5 no. 2. Cambridge, MA: Peabody Museum of Archaeology and Ethnology, Harvard University.

Tikal Reports (see TR. 12):
TR. 11:
Carr, Robert F., and James E. Hazard
1961   Map of the Ruins of Tikal, El Peten, Guatemala. In *Tikal Reports 1–11*, edited by E.M. Shook, W.R. Coe, V.L. Broman, and L. Satterthwaite, pp. iii–26. Facsimile Reissue of 1986 of Original Reports Published 1958–1961. Philadelphia: The University Museum, University of Pennsylvania.

TR. 23A:
Loten, H. Stanley
2002   *Miscellaneous Investigations in Central Tikal.* Philadelphia: University of Pennsylvania Museum of Archaeology and Anthropology.

TR. 23B:
Loten, H. Stanley
2017   *Miscellaneous Investigations in Central Tikal: Great Temples III, IV, V, and VI*. Philadelphia: University of Pennsylvania Museum of Archaeology and Anthropology.

TR. 23C:
Loten, H. Stanley
2018   *Miscellaneous Investigations in Central Tikal: The Plaza of the Seven Temples*. Philadelphia: University of Pennsylvania Museum of Archaeology and Anthropology.

Illustrations

FIGURE 1

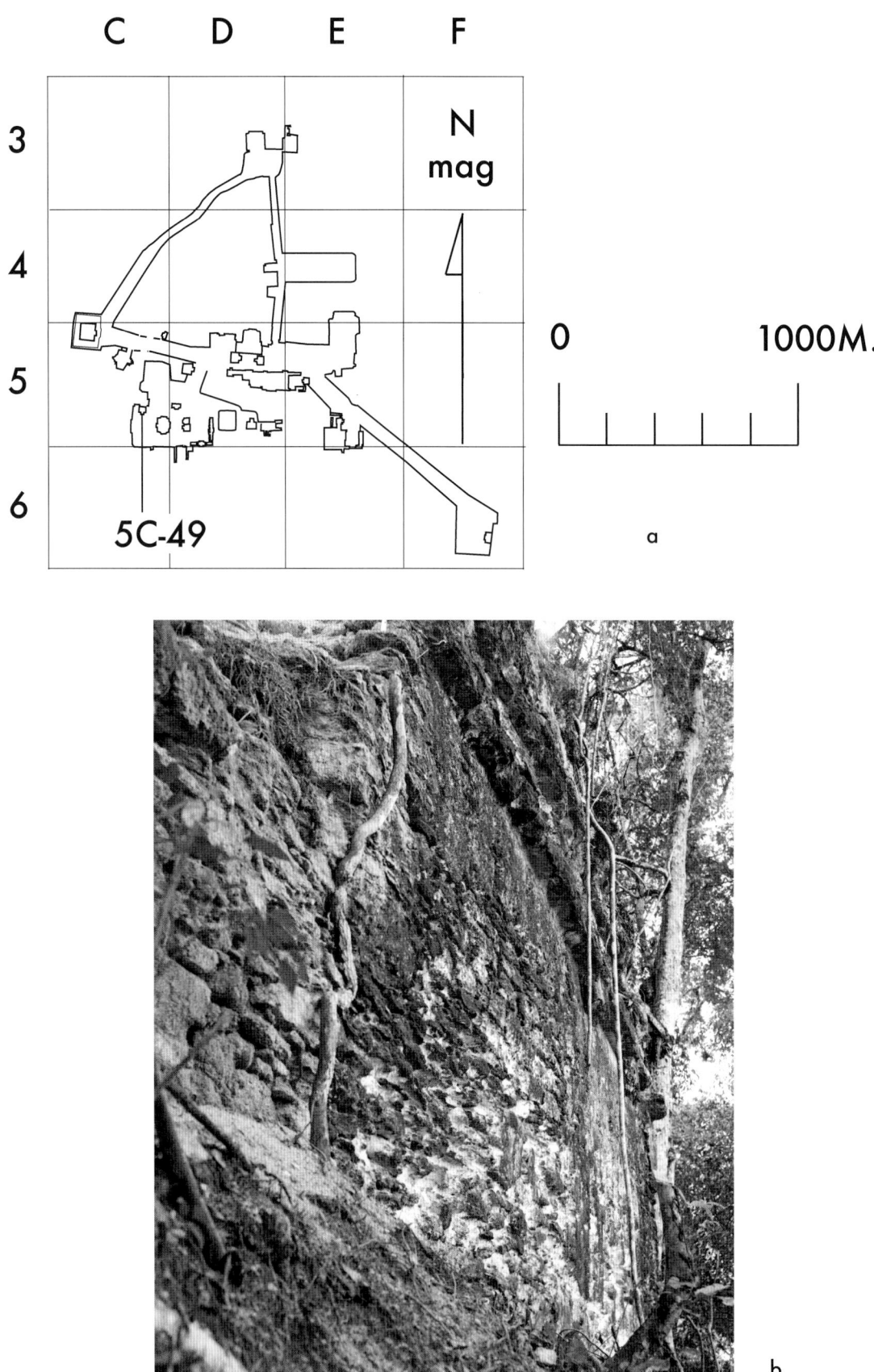

Str. 5C-49 Location and Photograph.
a. Location map after TR. 11 (scale 1:25,000). *b*. View of N facade.

FIGURE 2

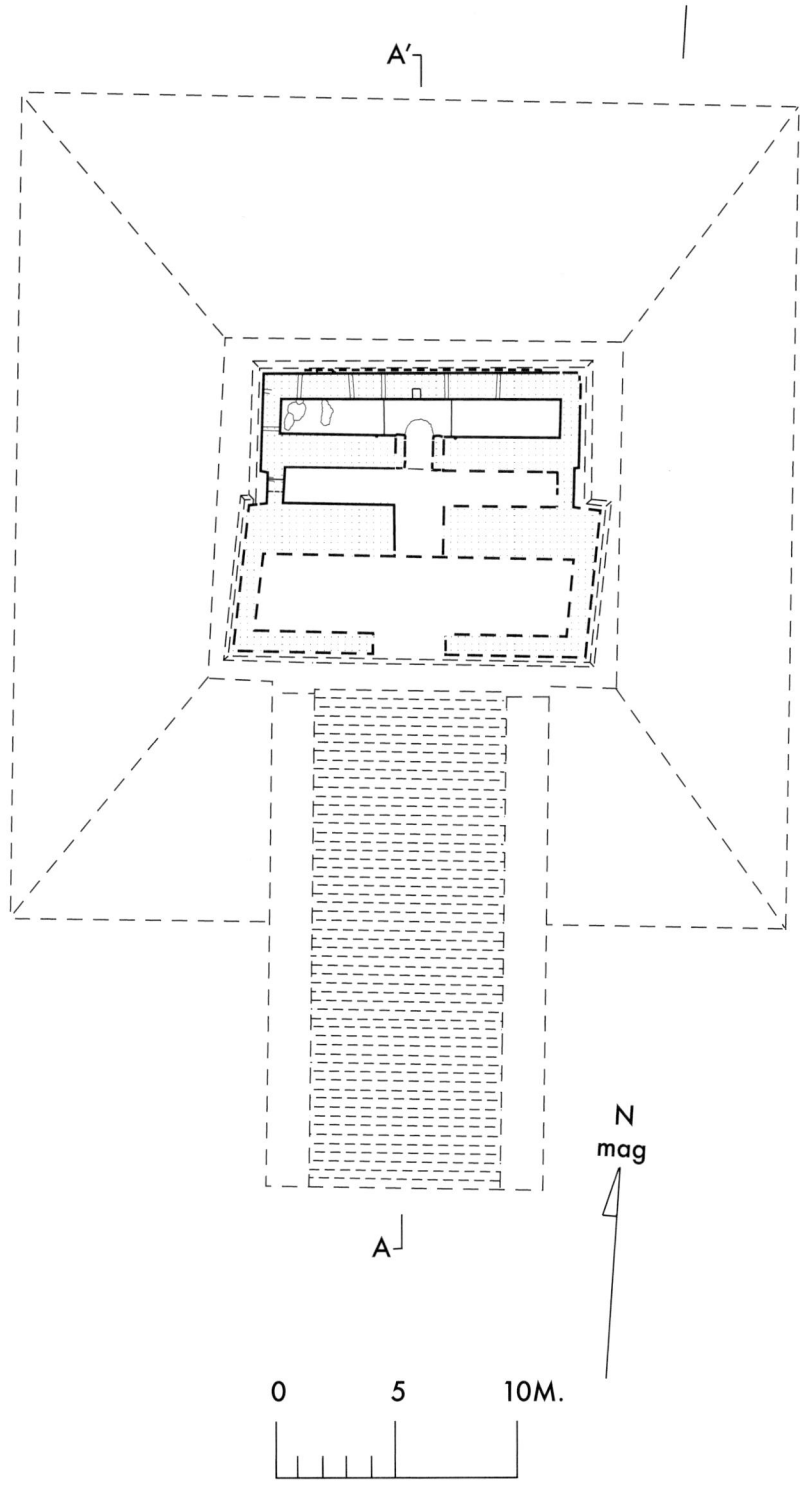

Str. 5C-49 Plan (scale 1:300).

FIGURE 3

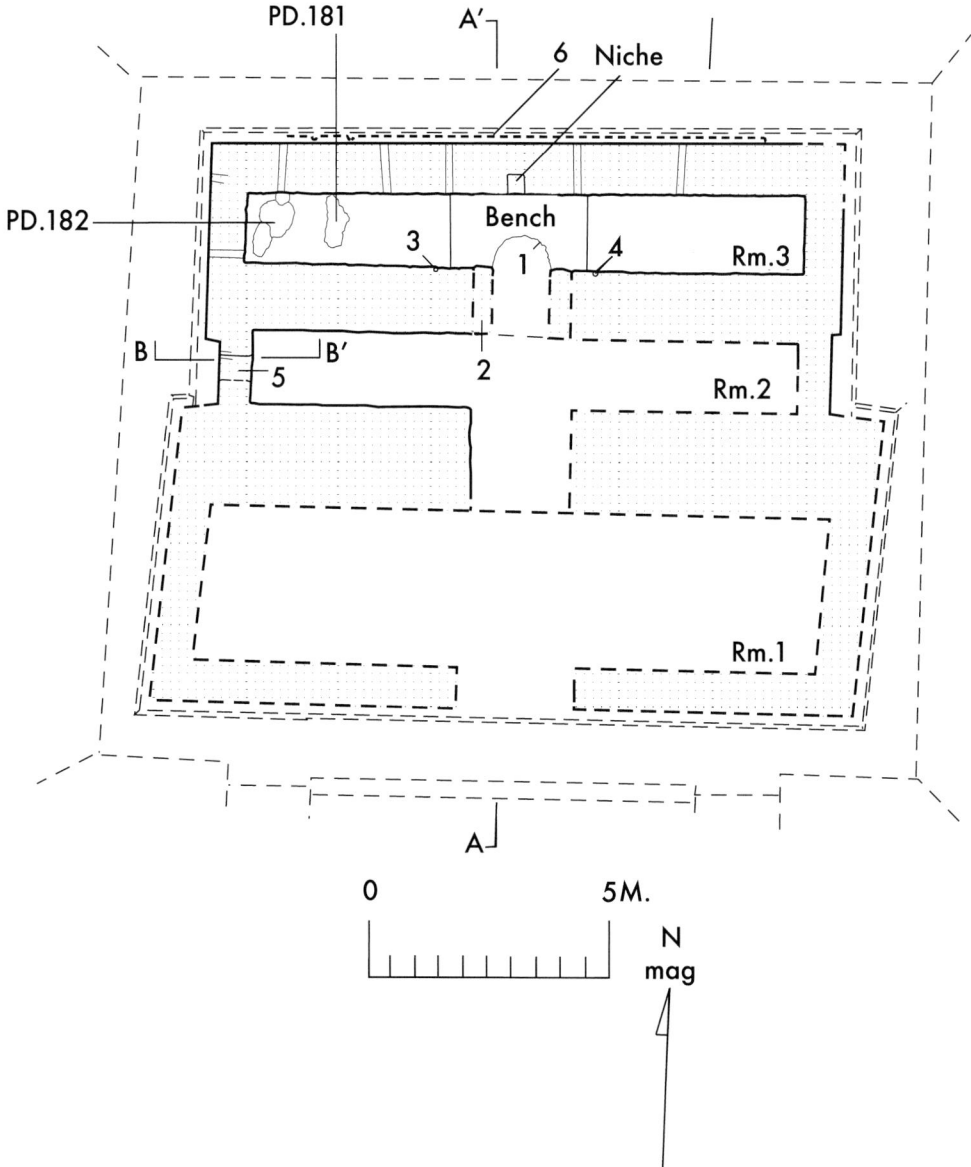

Str. 5C-49 Building Plan (scale 1:150).
1, Chop-line in bench. *2*, Jamb block. *3*, Cord holder 2. *4*, Cord holder 1. *5*, Vent. *6*, Vertically grooved stucco.

FIGURE 4

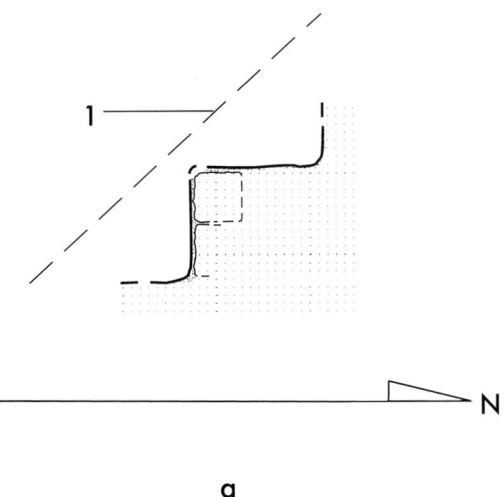

a

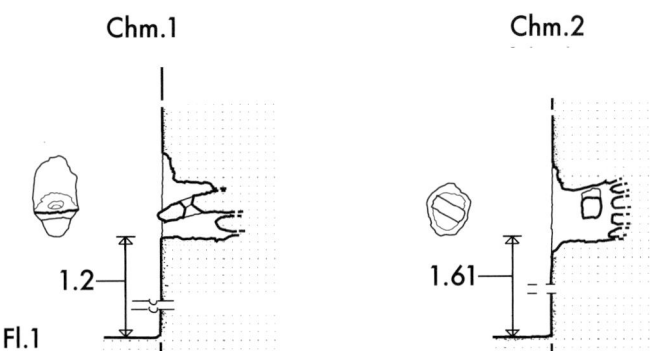

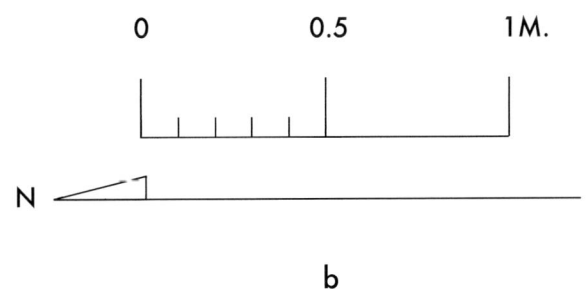

b

Str. 5C-49 Details (scale 1:20).
a. Stair detail. *1*, Line of balustrade. *b*. Cord holder details.

FIGURE 5

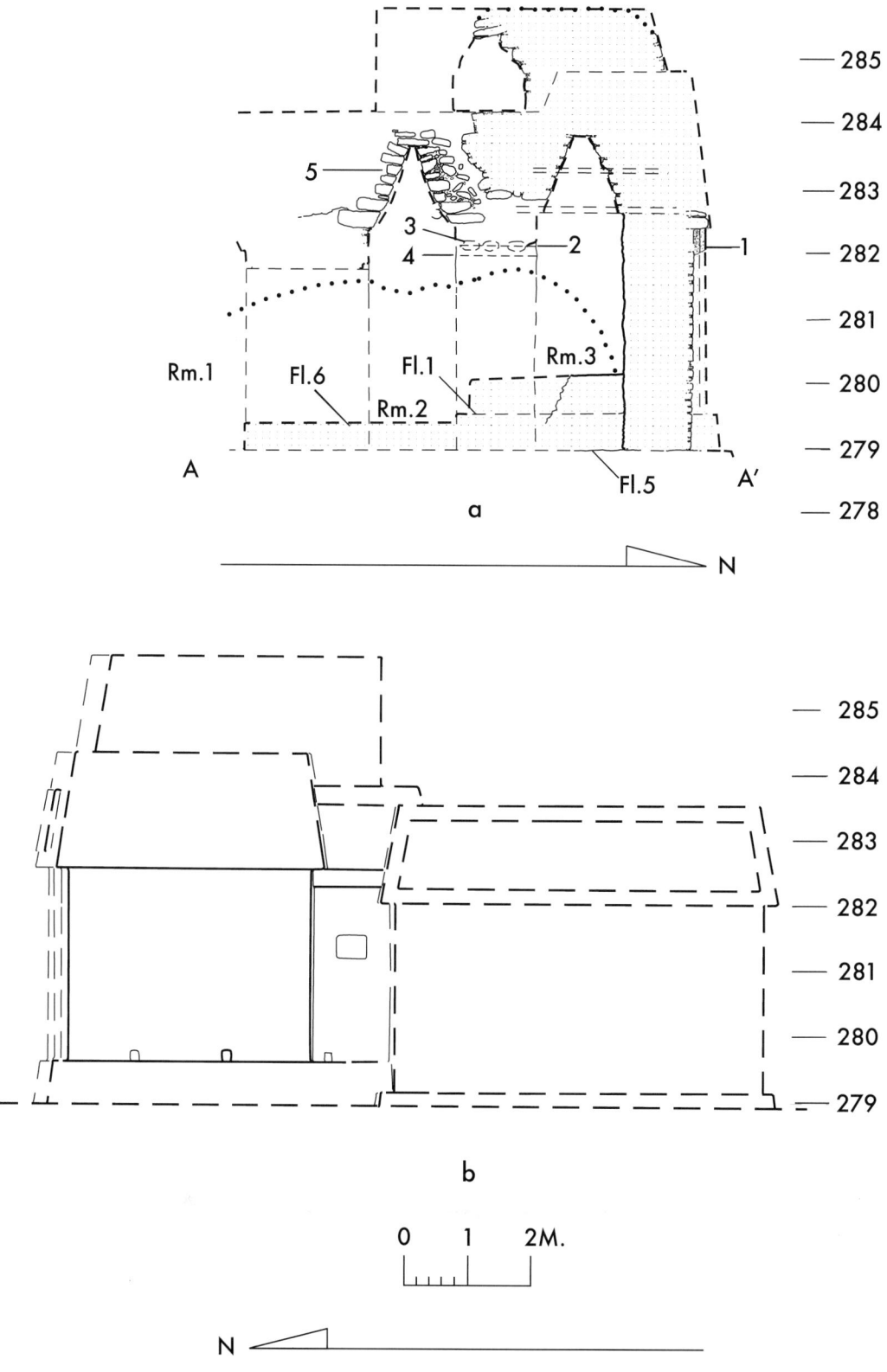

Str. 5C-49 Superstructure (scale 1:100).
 a. Section/profile A-A' superstructure. *1*, Vertically grooved stucco. *2*, Top of E jamb block. *3*, Lintel beam socket impressions. *4*, Primary lintel bed level. *5*, Vault details off-section.
 b. W elevation superstructure.

FIGURE 6

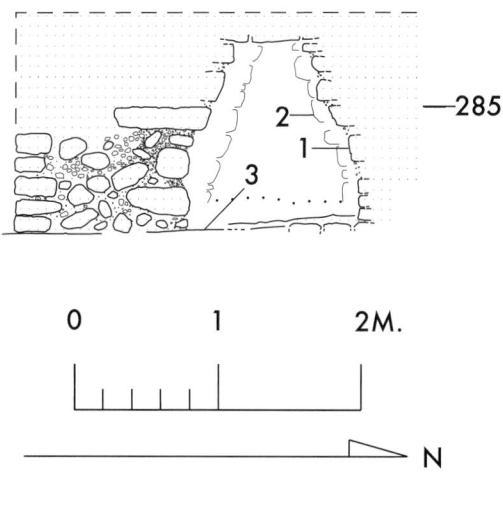

a

b

Str. 5C-49 Roof Structure.
a. Section/profile (scale 1:50). *1*, Profile 1.5 m W of centerline (scale 1:50). *2*, Profile 3.5 m W of centerline. *3*, Roof plaster. *b*. View of roof-structure vault.

FIGURE 7

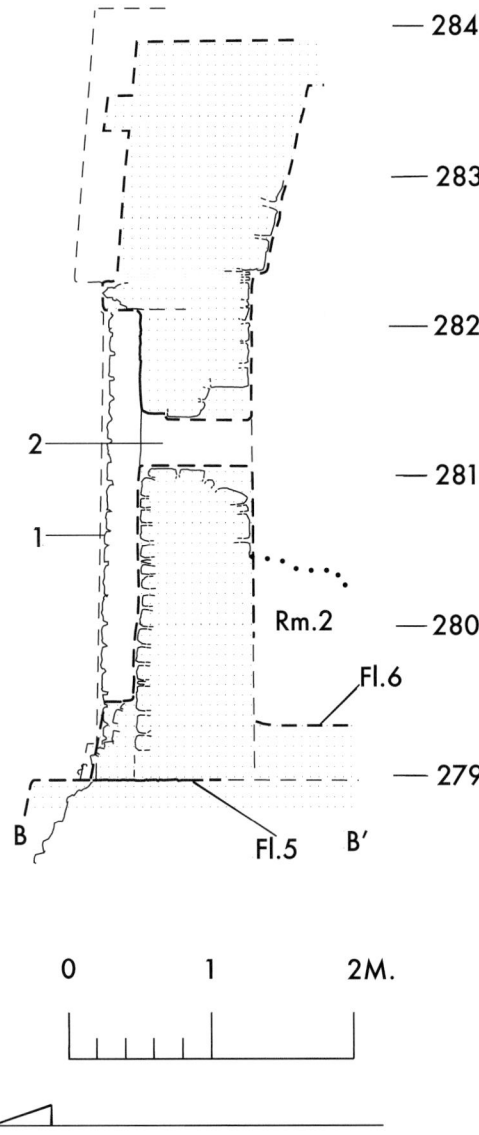

Str. 5C-49 Section/Profile B-B' (scale 1:50).
1, Wall profile to N of side inset. *2*, Vent.

FIGURE 8

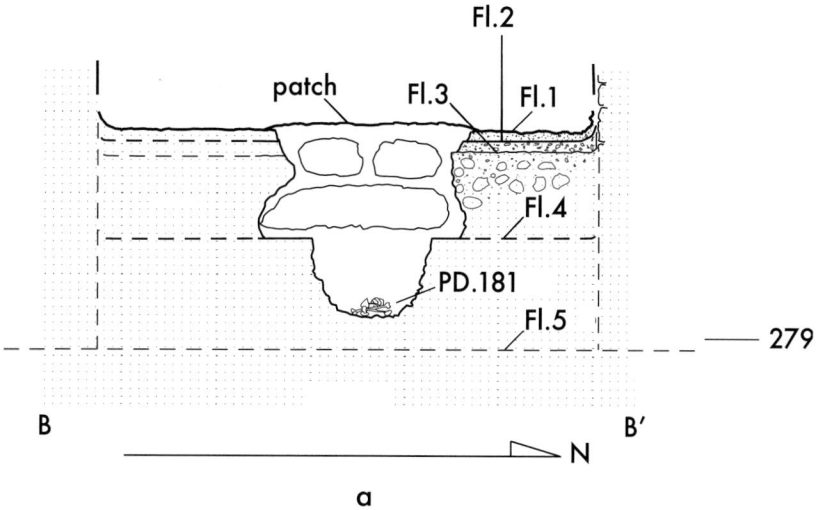

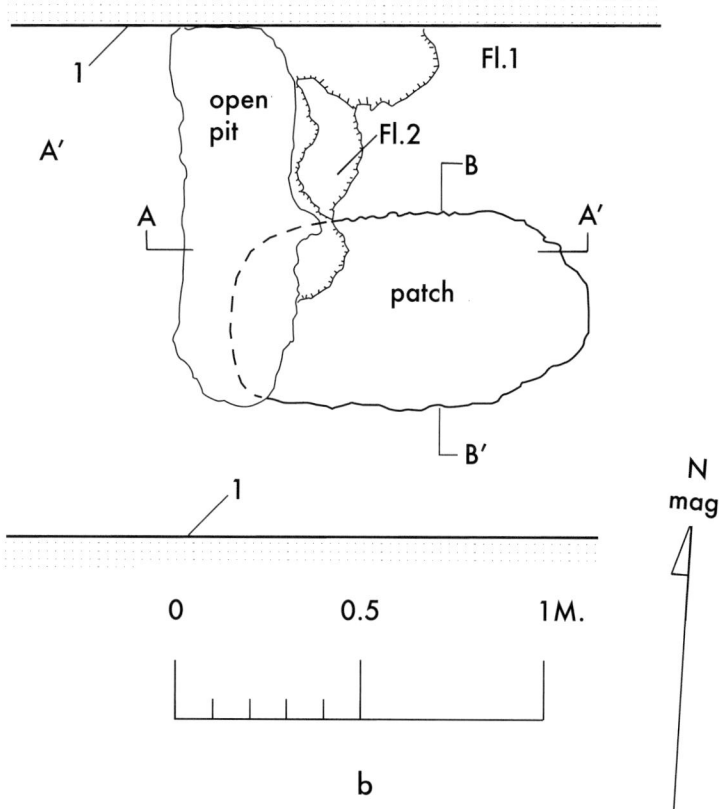

Str. 5C-49 PD. 181 (scale 1:20).
a. Section B-B'. *b*. Plan. *1*, Wall line.

FIGURE 9

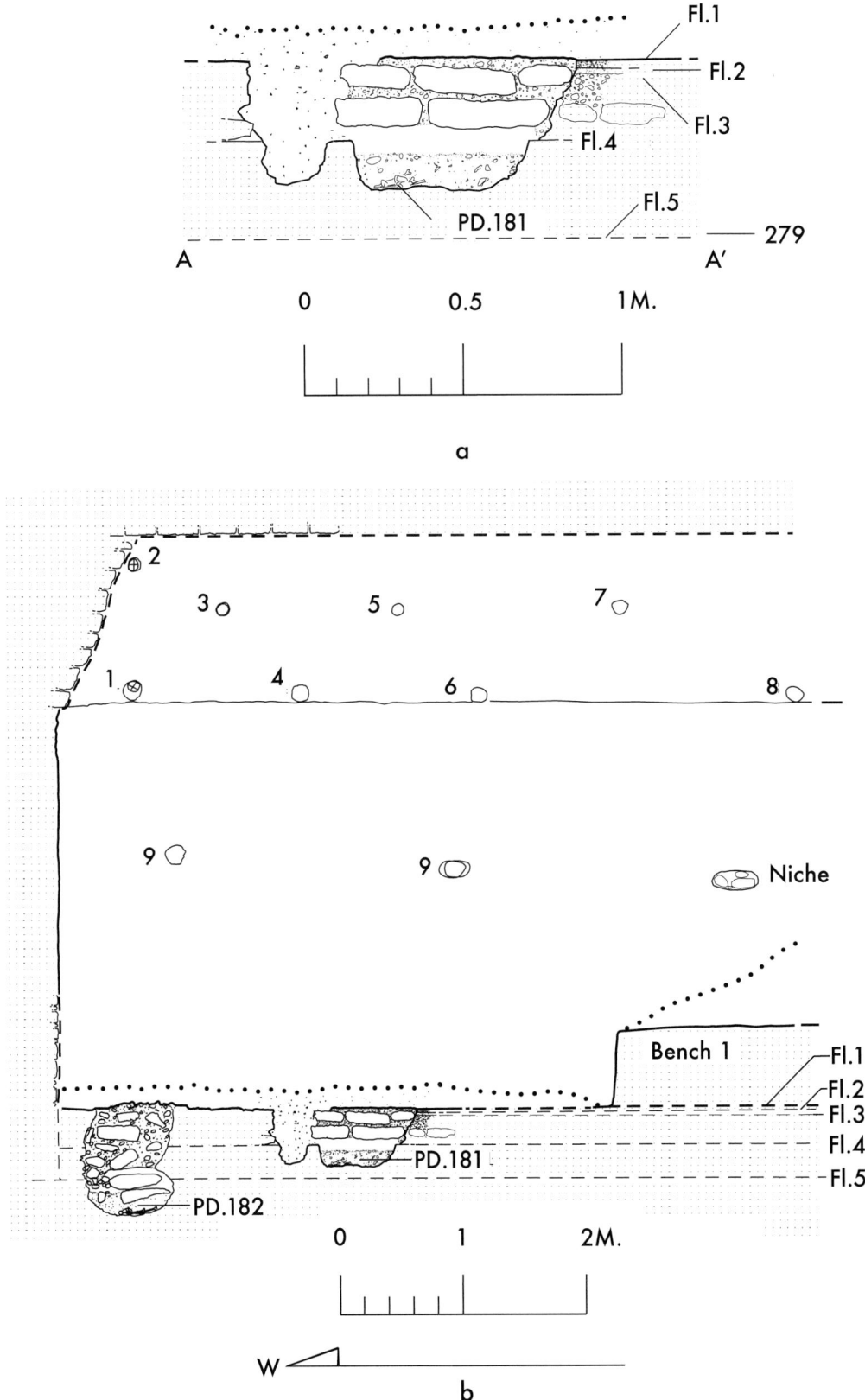

Str. 5C-49 PD. 181 and 182.
a. Section/profile A-A' (scale 1:20). *b*. Partial elevation Rm. 3 (scale 1:50). *1–8*, Vault-beam holes. *9*, Subspring-beam holes.

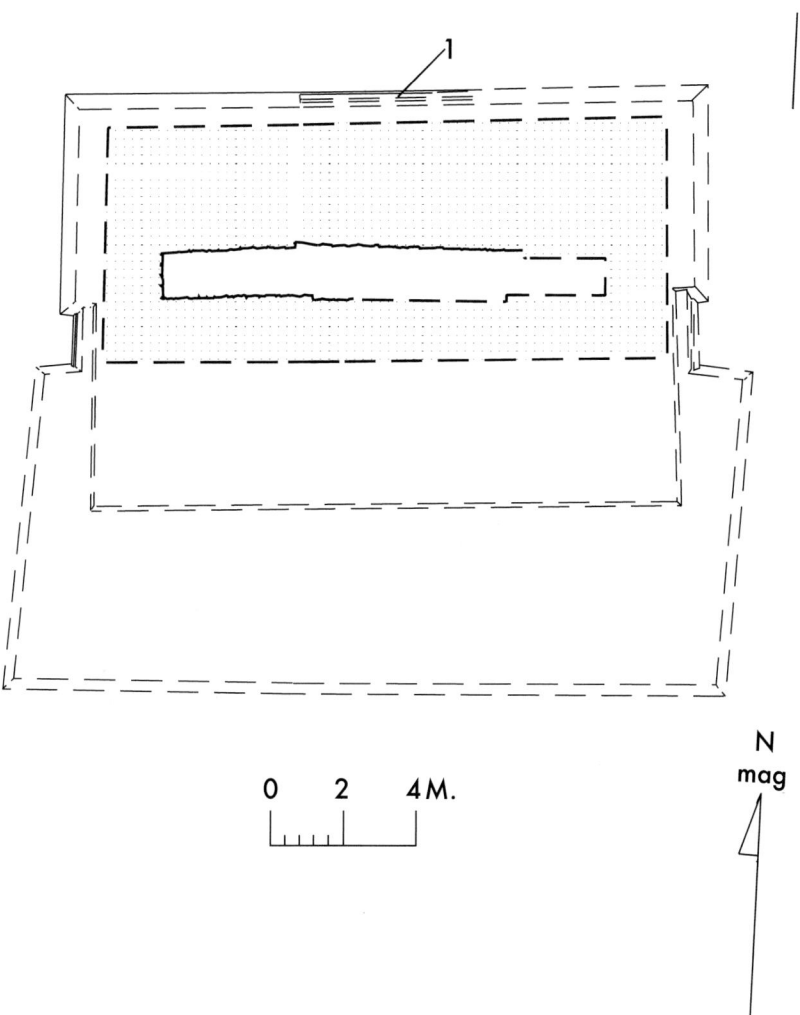

FIGURE 10

Str. 5C-49 Roof-Structure Plan (scale 1:150).
1, Upper-zone panel.

FIGURE 11

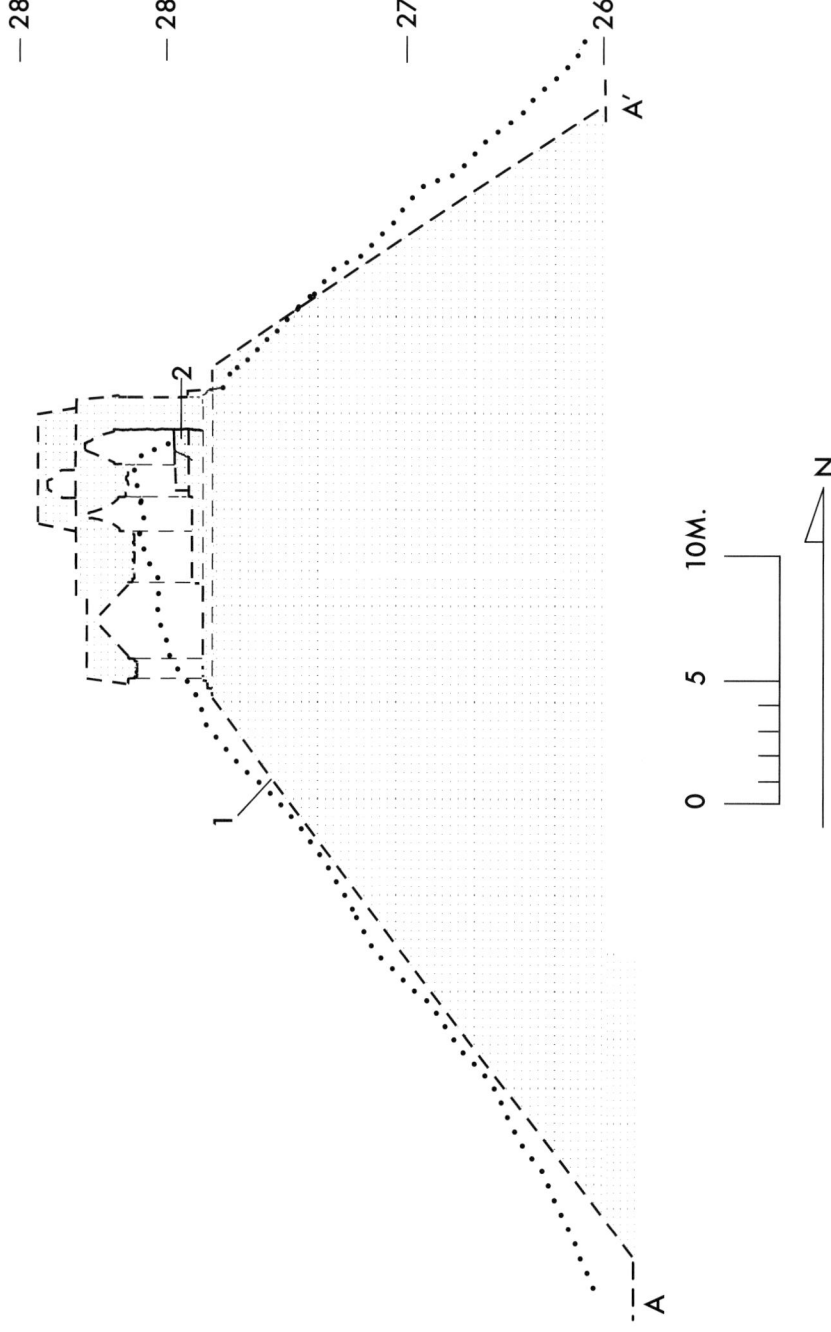

Str. 5C-49 Section/Profile A-A' (scale 1:300).
1, Estimated line of stair. 2, Axial bench.

FIGURE 12

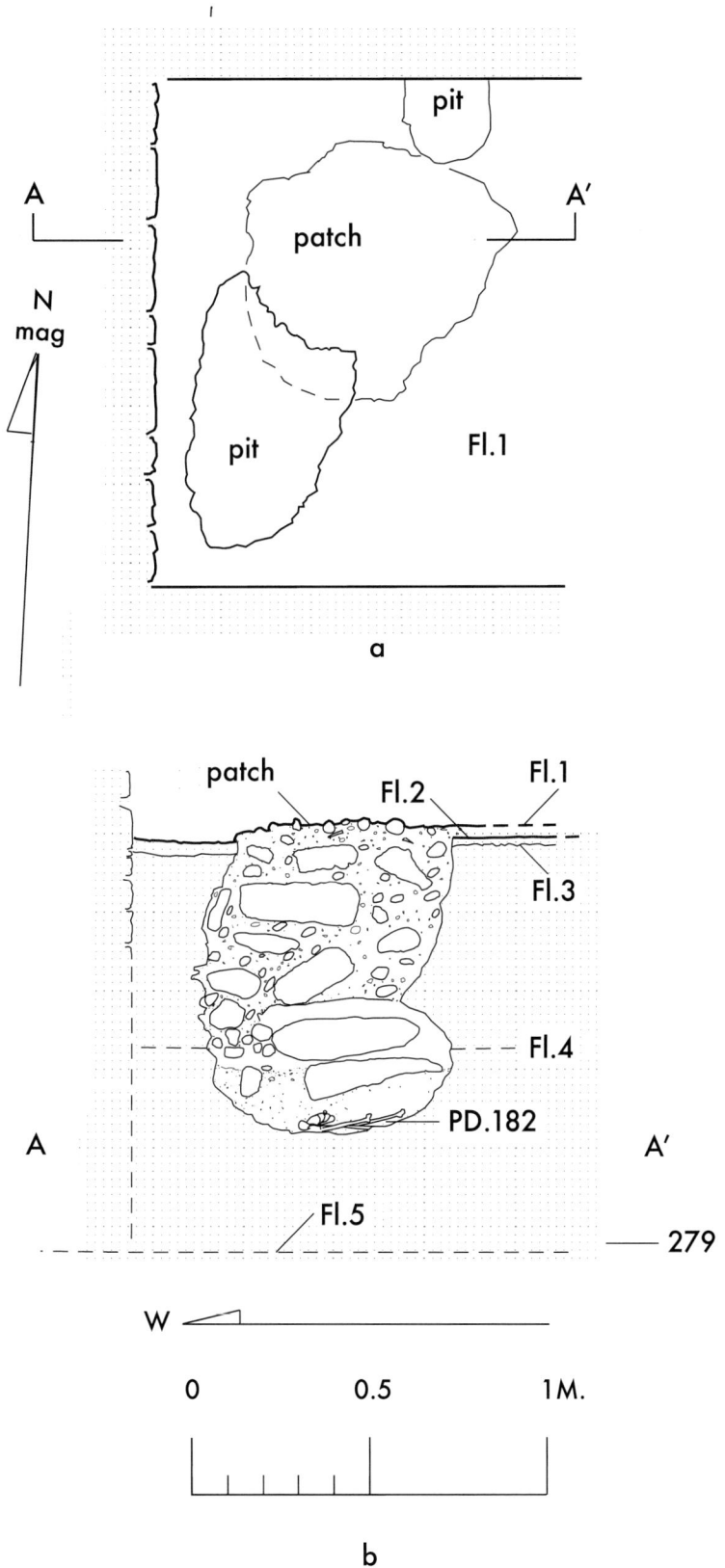

Str. 5C-49 PD. 182 (scale 1:20).
a. Plan. *b*. Section A-A'.

FIGURE 13

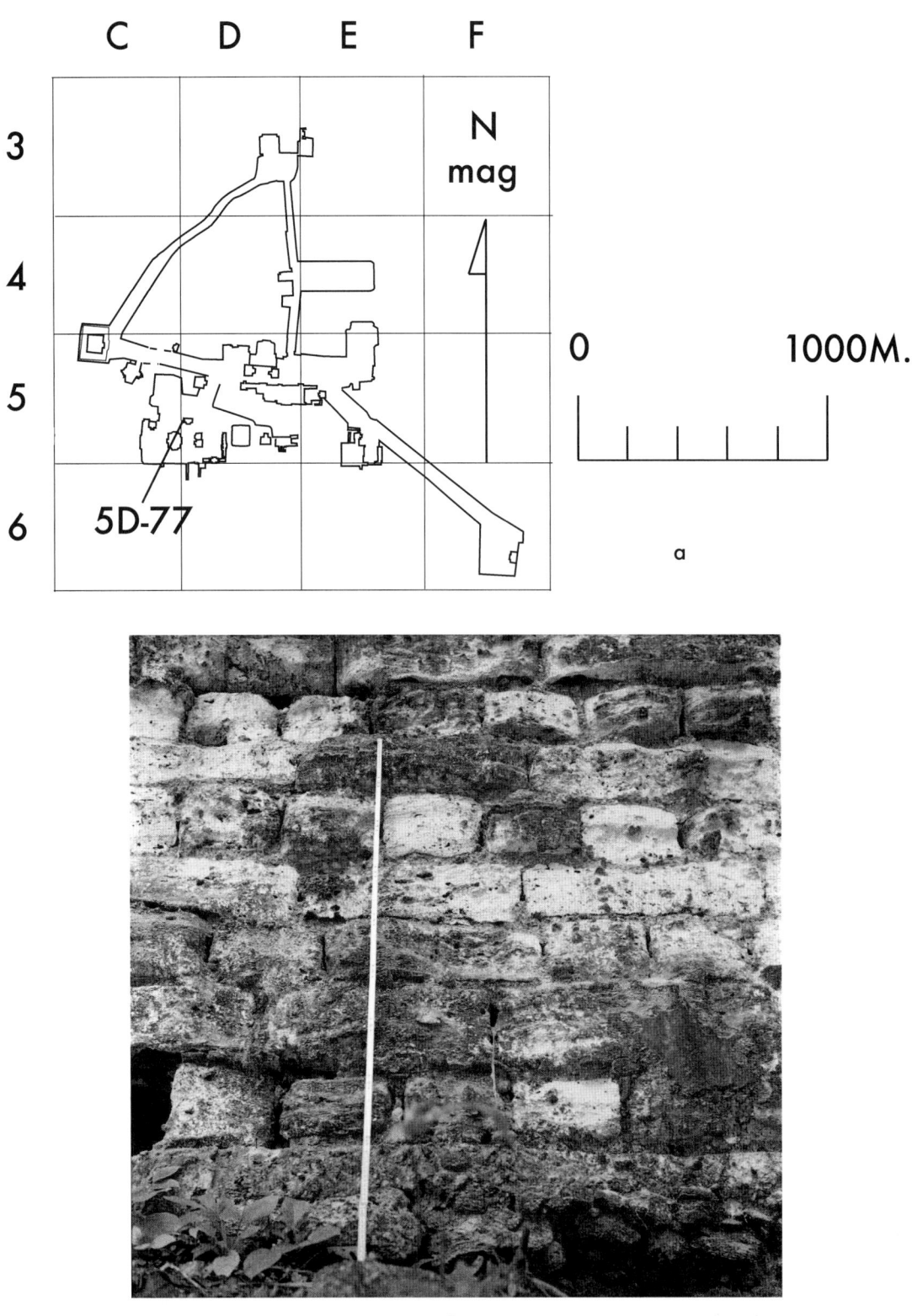

Str. 5D-77 Location and Photograph.
a. Location map after TR. 11 (scale 1:25,000). *b.* View of exterior rear wall masonry.

FIGURE 14

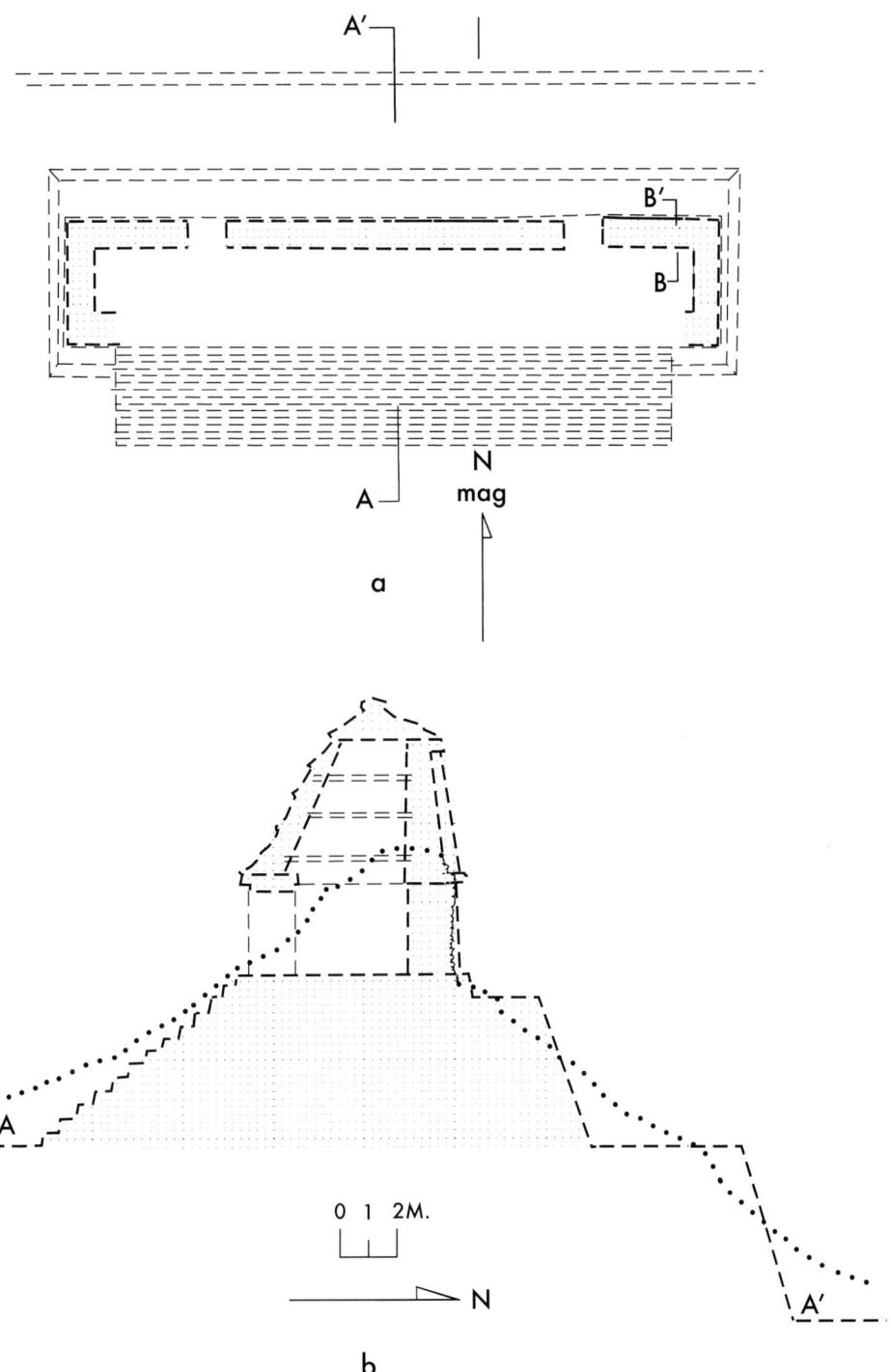

Str. 5D-77 Plan and Section.
a. Plan (scale 1:250). *b*. Section/profile A-A' (scale 1:200).

FIGURE 15

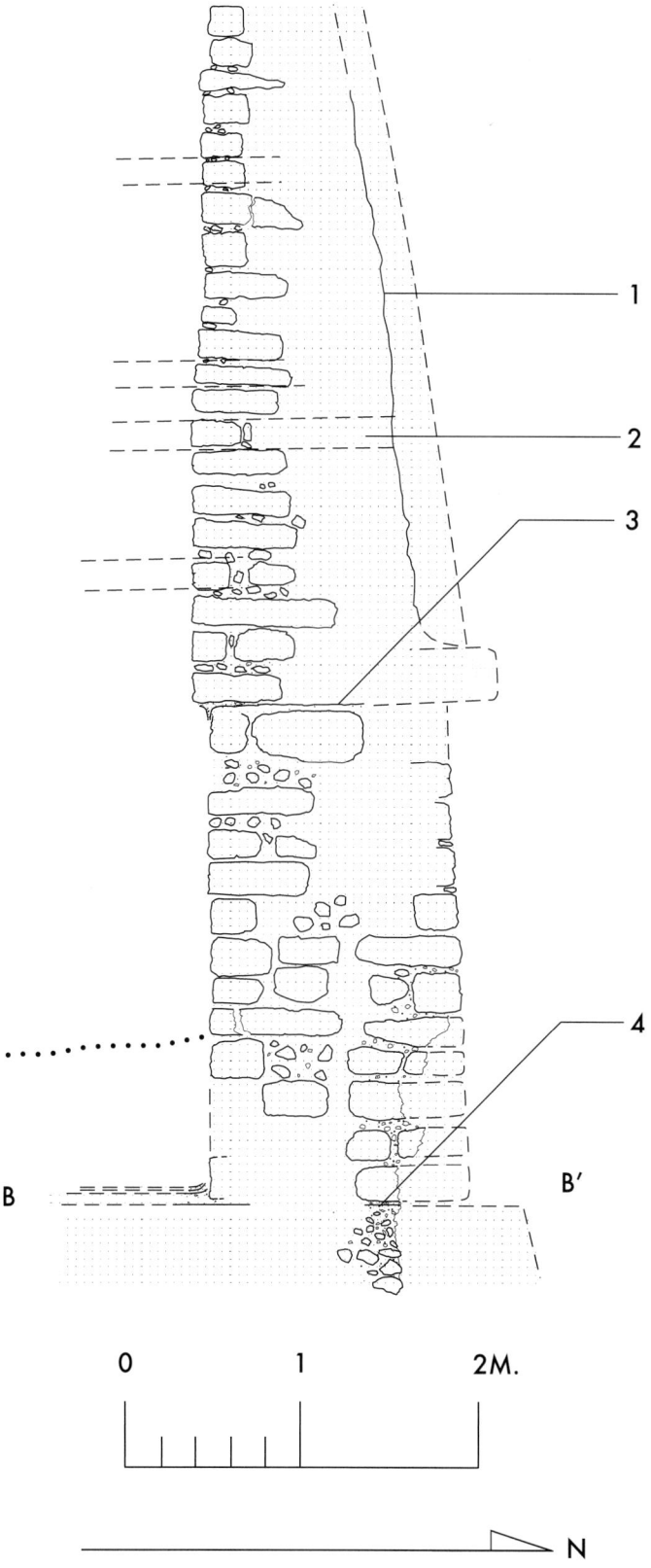

Str. 5D-77 Section/Profile B-B' (scale 1:40).
1, Vault-back surface. *2*, Assumed vent. *3*, Wall-top level (rough mortar). *4*, Building platform top surface.

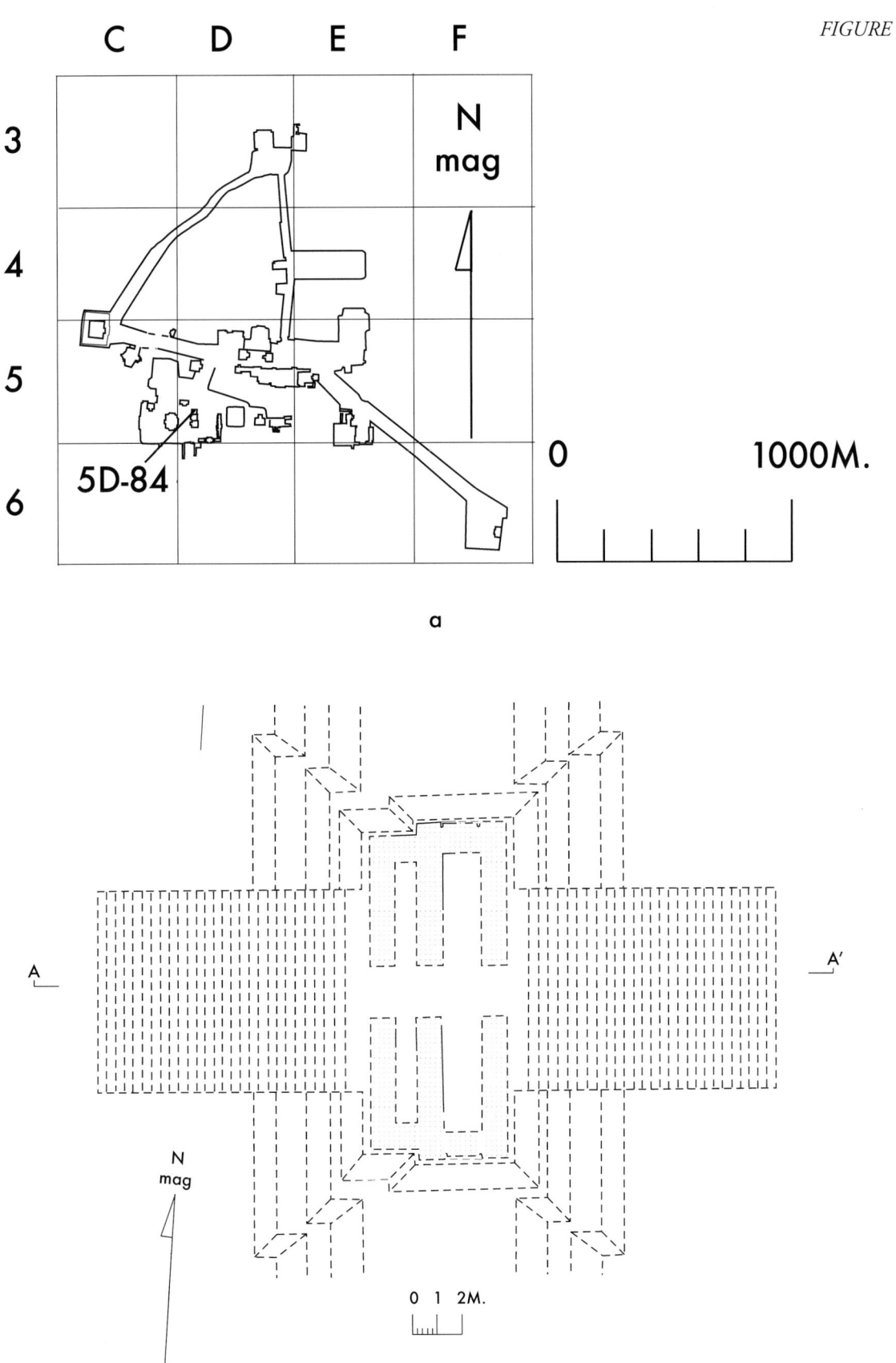

Str. 5D-84 Location and Plan.
a. Location map after TR. 11 (scale 1:25,000). b. Plan (scale 1:200).

FIGURE 17

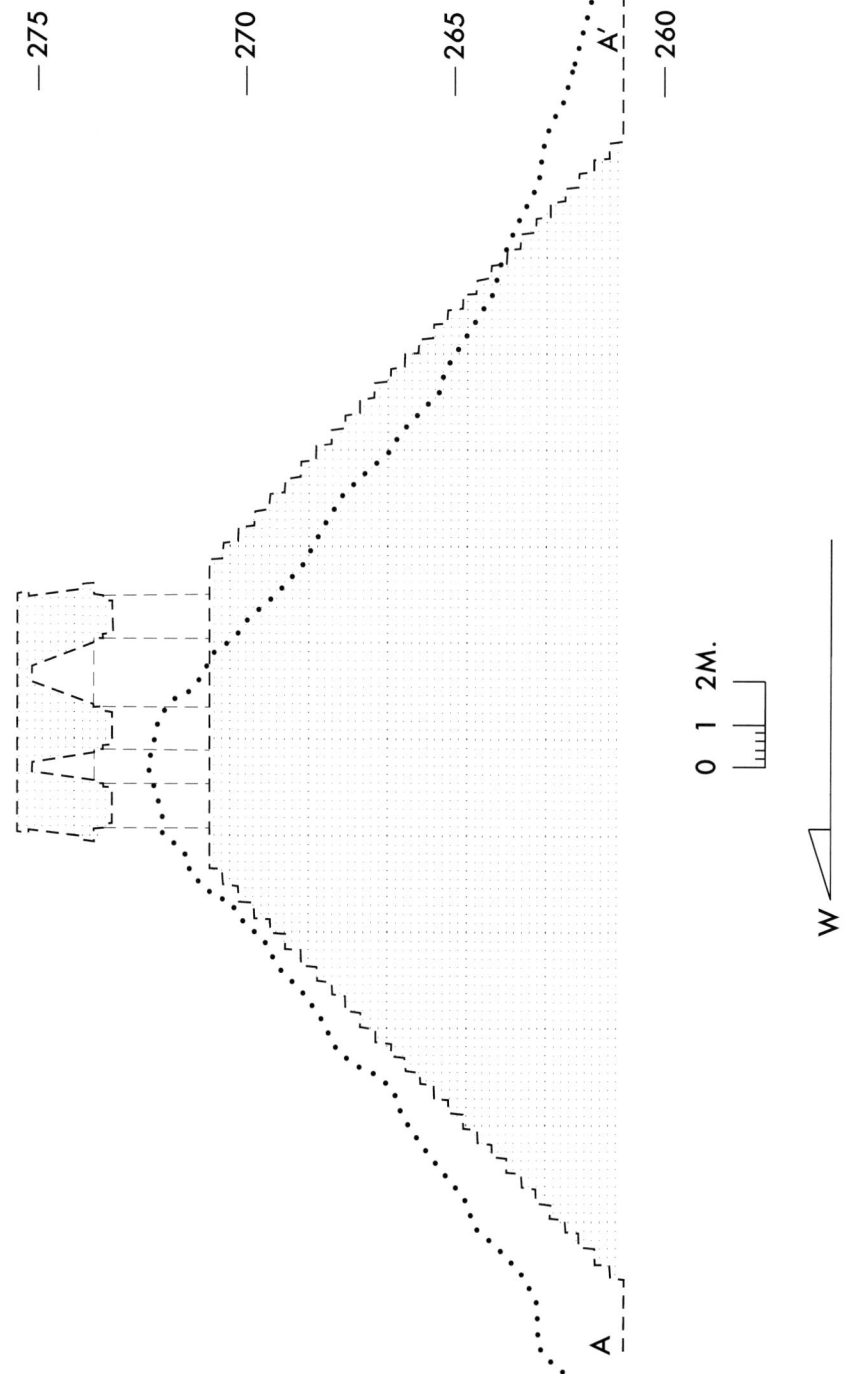

Str. 5D-84 Section/Profile A-A' (scale 1:175).

FIGURE 18

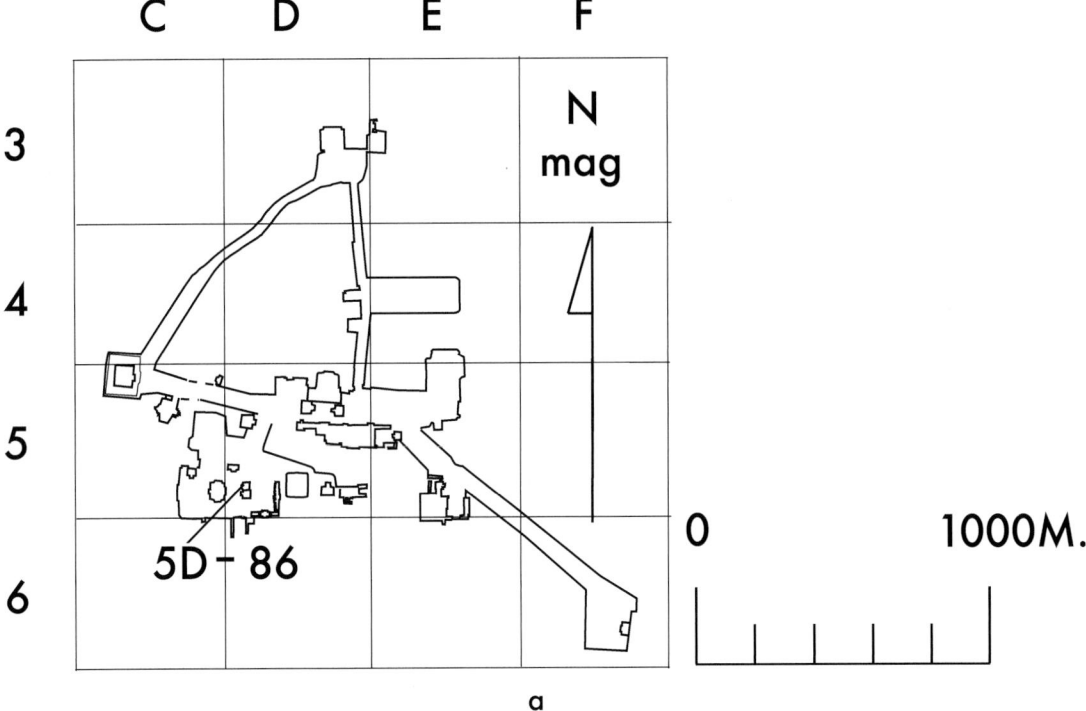

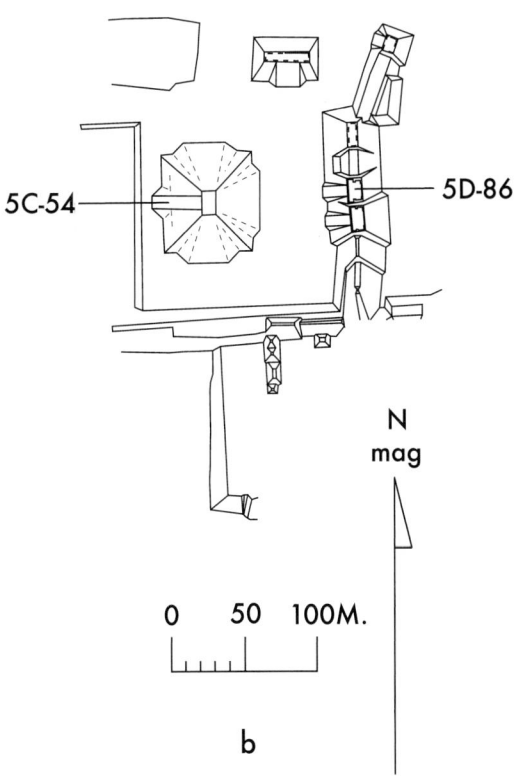

Str. 5D-86 Location.
a. Location map after TR. 11 (scale 1:25,000).
b. Location map after TR. 11 (scale 1:5,000).

FIGURE 19

Str. 5D-86 Photographs.
a. View of Rm. 2 looking N. *b*. View of N facade.

FIGURE 20

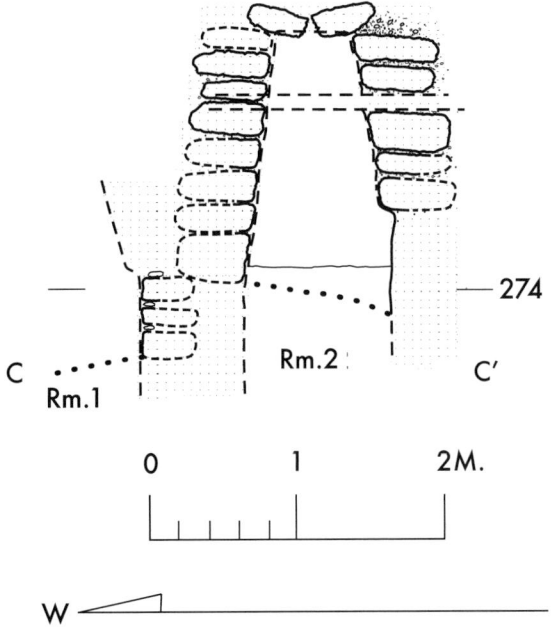

Str. 5D-86 Rm. 2 Vault.
a. Vault section/profile C-C' (scale 1:50) *b*. View of Rm. 2 vault N end.

FIGURE 21

Str. 5D-86 Photographs.
a. View of building looking N. *b*. View of wall section at N end of Rm. 1, looking E.

FIGURE 22

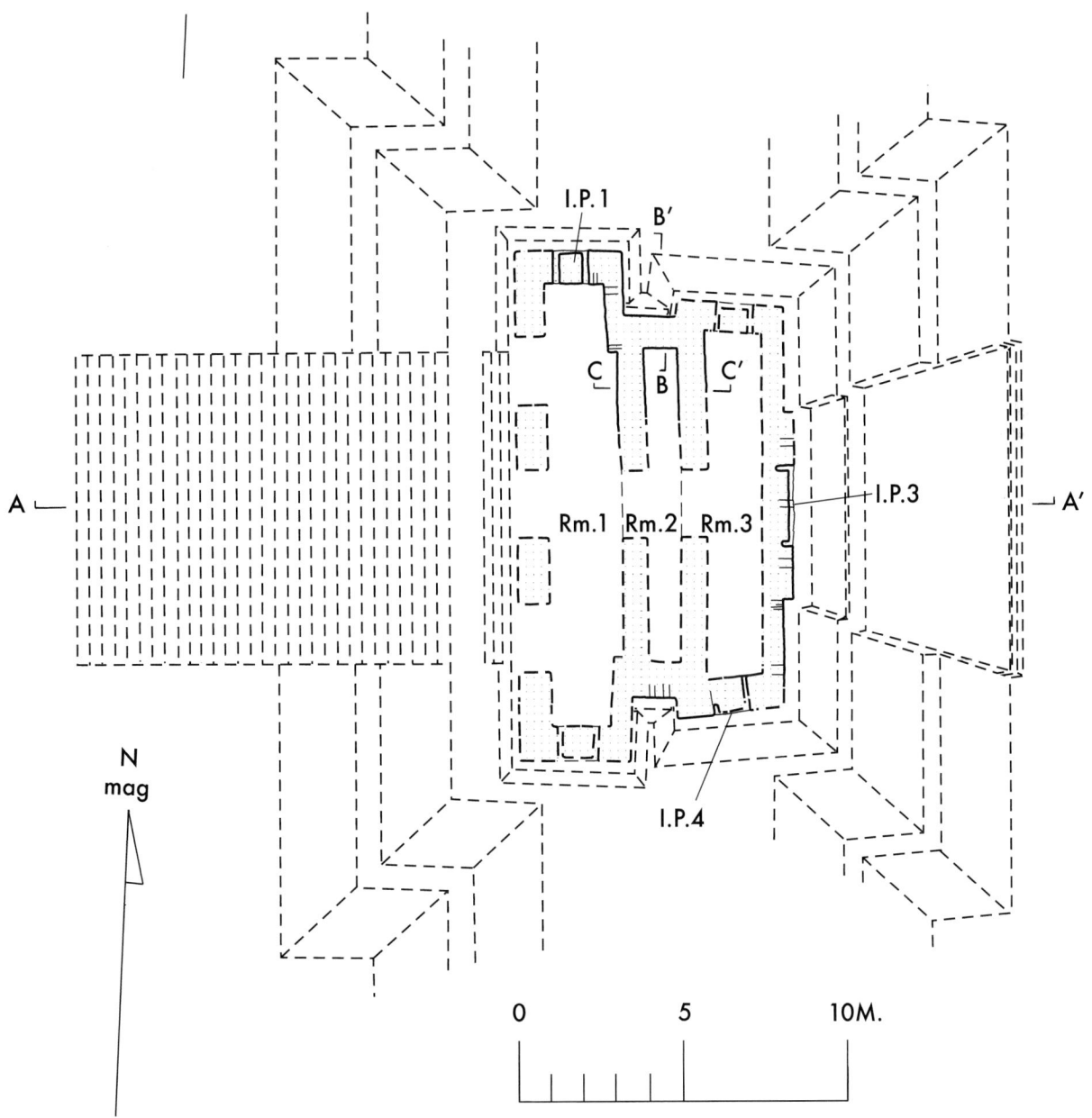

Str. 5D-86 Plan (scale 1:200). Substructure format conjectural.

FIGURE 23

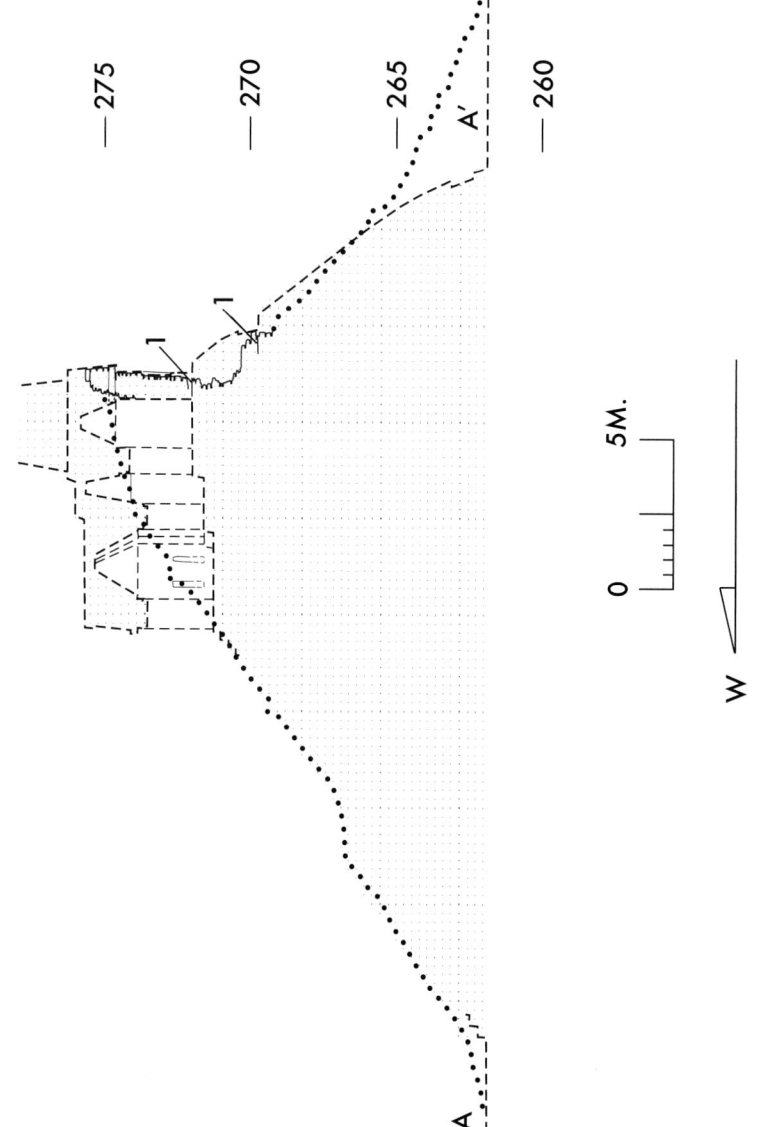

Str. 5D-86 Section/Profile A-A' (scale 1:250). *1*, Hard plaster surface.

FIGURE 24

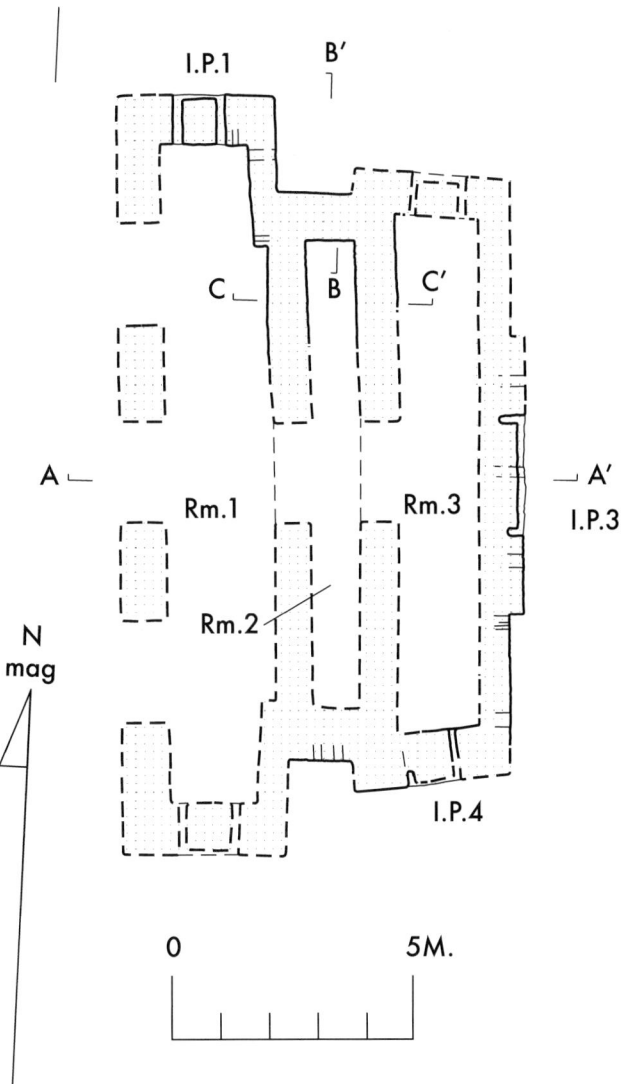

Str. 5D-86 Building Plan (scale 1:150).

Str. 5D-86 Stucco Modeling.
a. Wall section B-B' at N side inset. *1*, Primary plaster with red paint. *2*, Stucco relief with red paint in grooves. *3*, Thin plaster with red paint turning onto base of stucco relief. *4*, Roughly finished mortar application concealing stucco relief. *5*, Primary plaster with red paint. *6*, Vent opening into Rm. 1. *7*, Debris profile. *8*, Hard plaster roof surface. *b*. Stucco relief at N side inset. *1*, Vault-back, plastered and red-painted. *2*, Modeled stucco, red paint in grooves. *3*, Red paint. *4*, Red paint. *5*, Dark gray plaster.

FIGURE 25

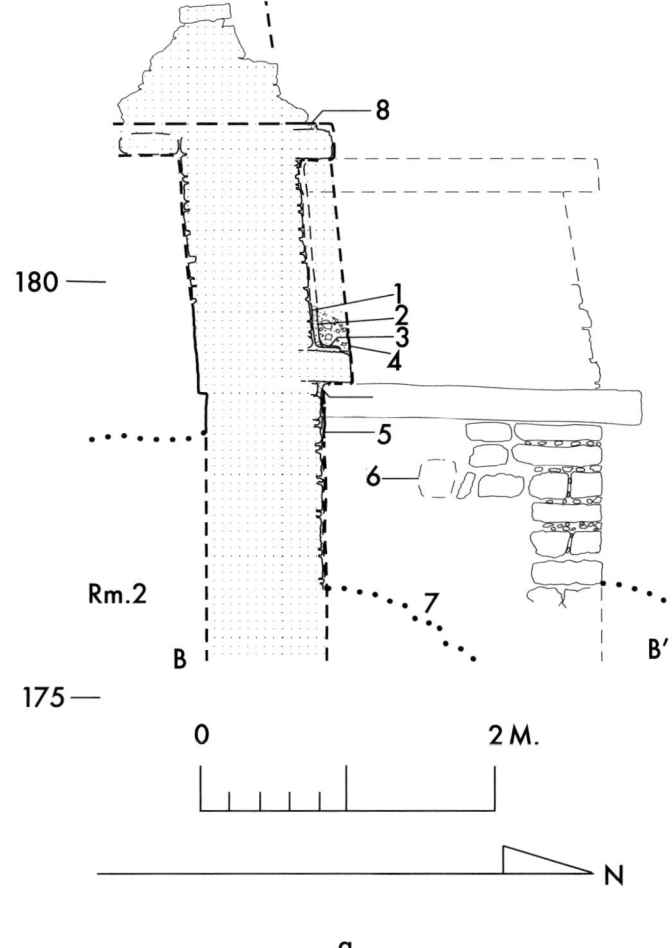

a

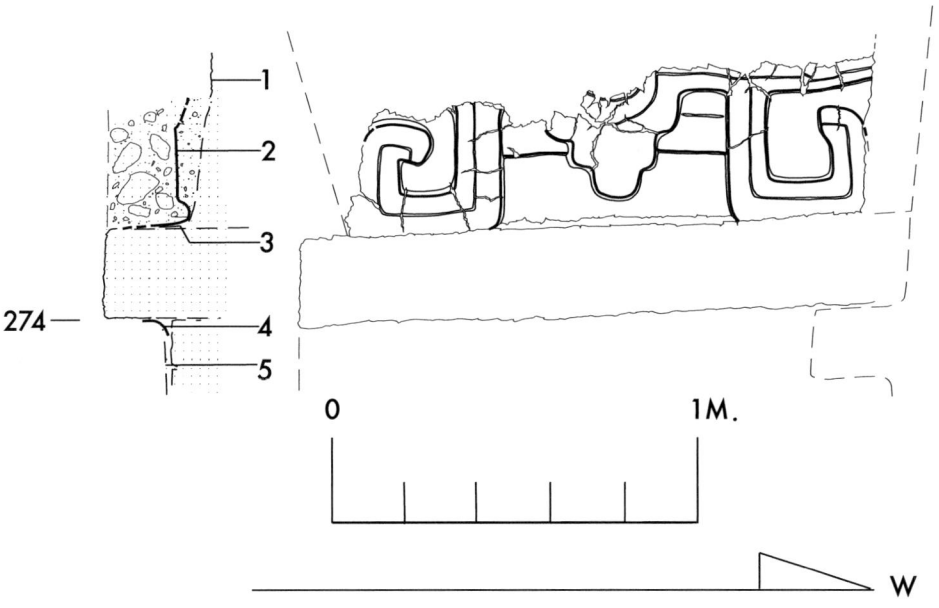

b

FIGURE 26

a

b

Str. 5D-86 Stucco Modeling.
a. View of N side inset. *b*. View of stucco modeling.

FIGURE 27

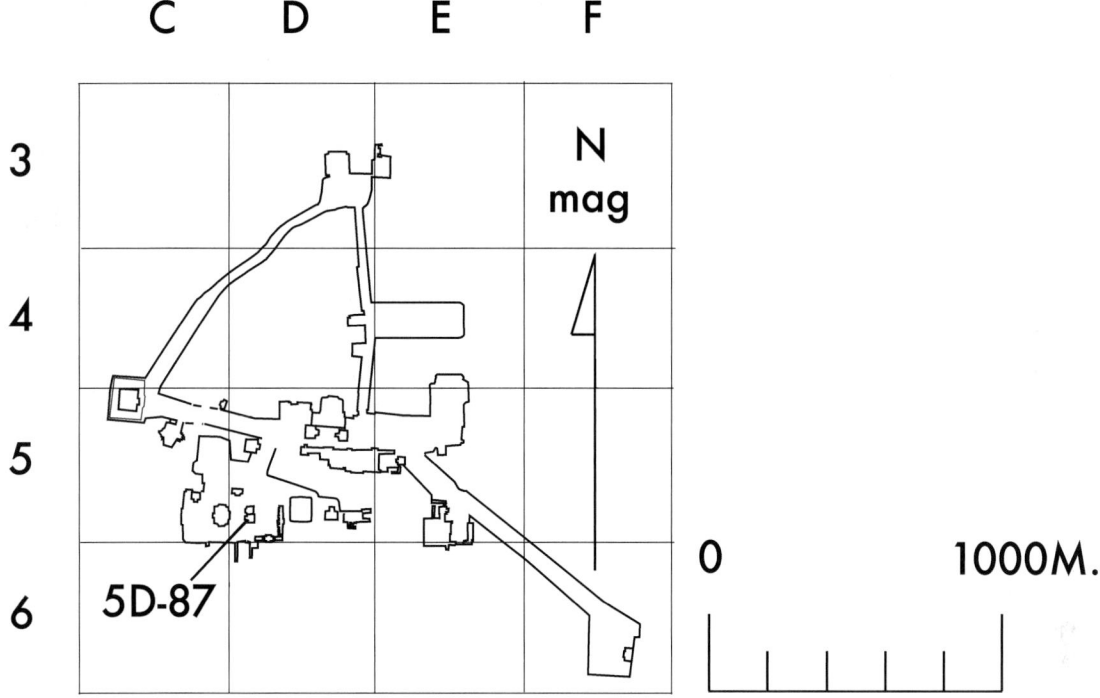

a

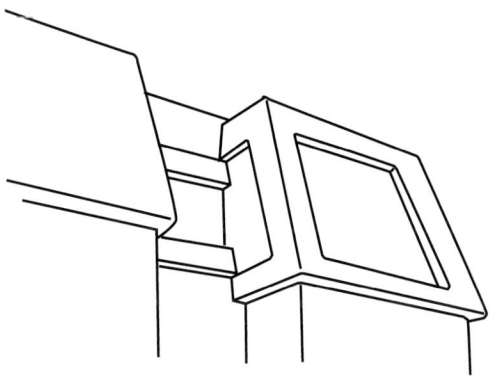

b

Str. 5D-87 Location and Perspective.
a. Location map after TR. 11 (scale 1:25,000).
b. Perspective vignette of upper zone NW.

FIGURE 28

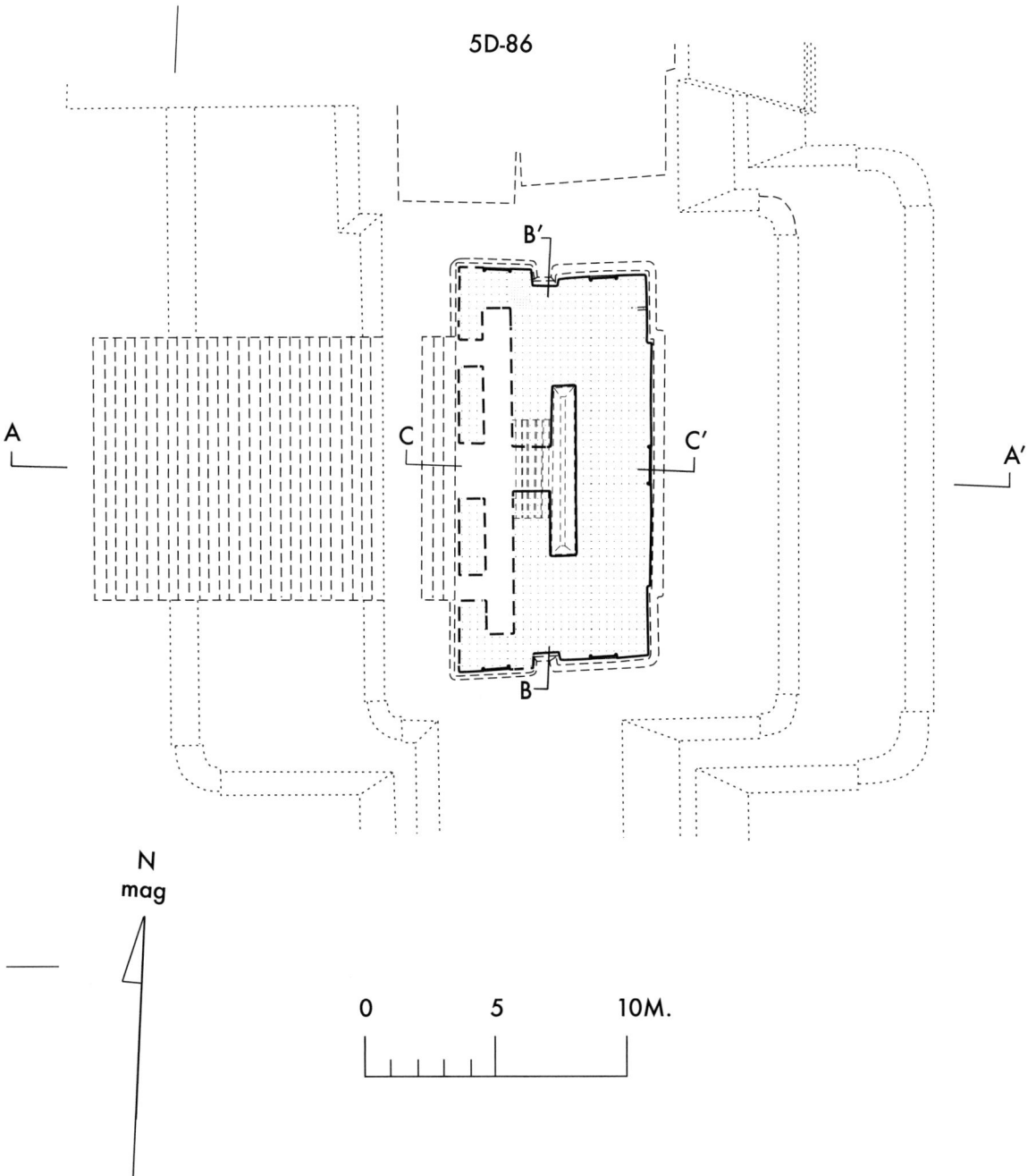

Str. 5D-87 Plan (scale 1:250).

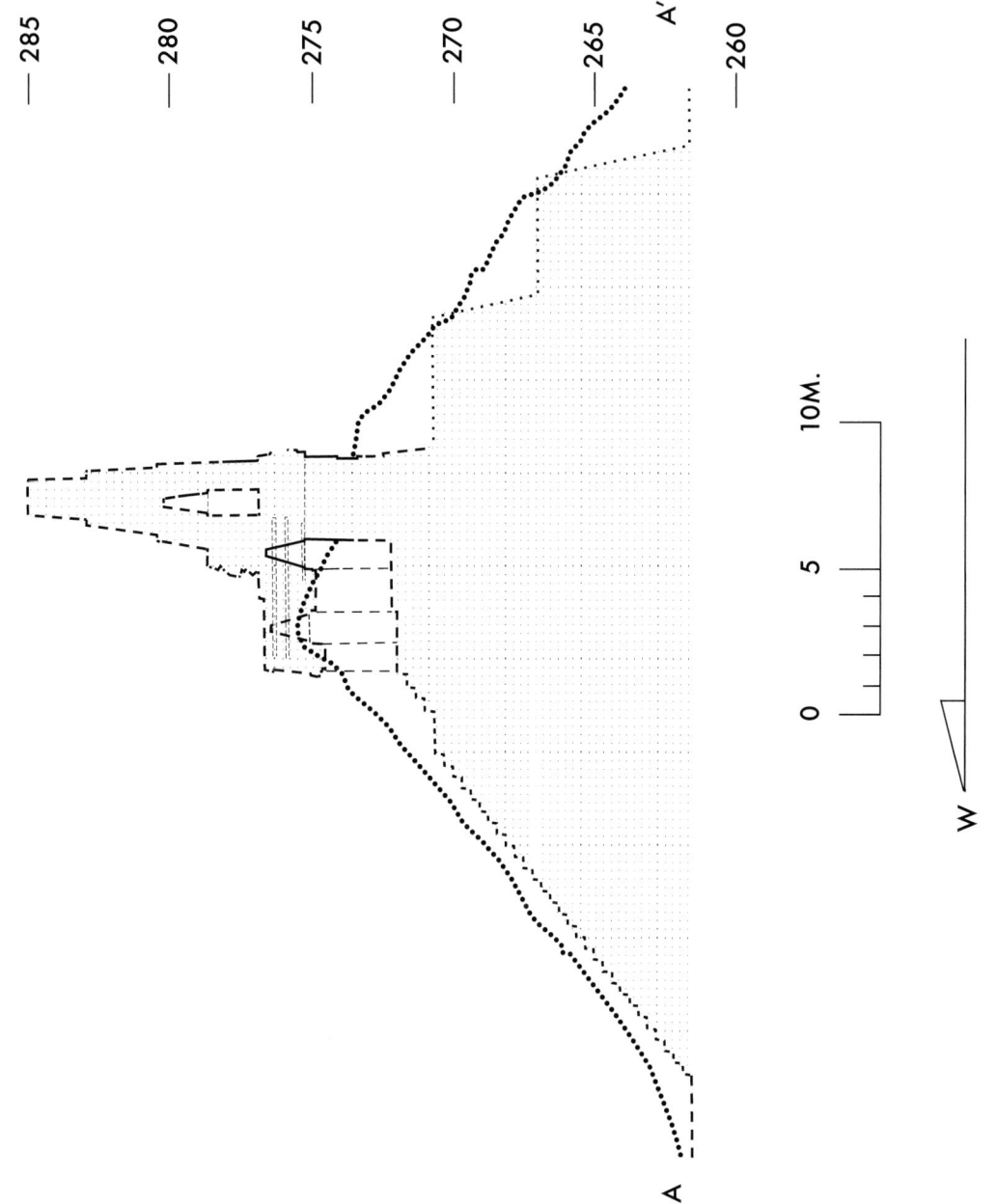

Str. 5D-87 Section/Profile A-A' (scale 1:250). Lower substructure conjectural.

FIGURE 29

FIGURE 30

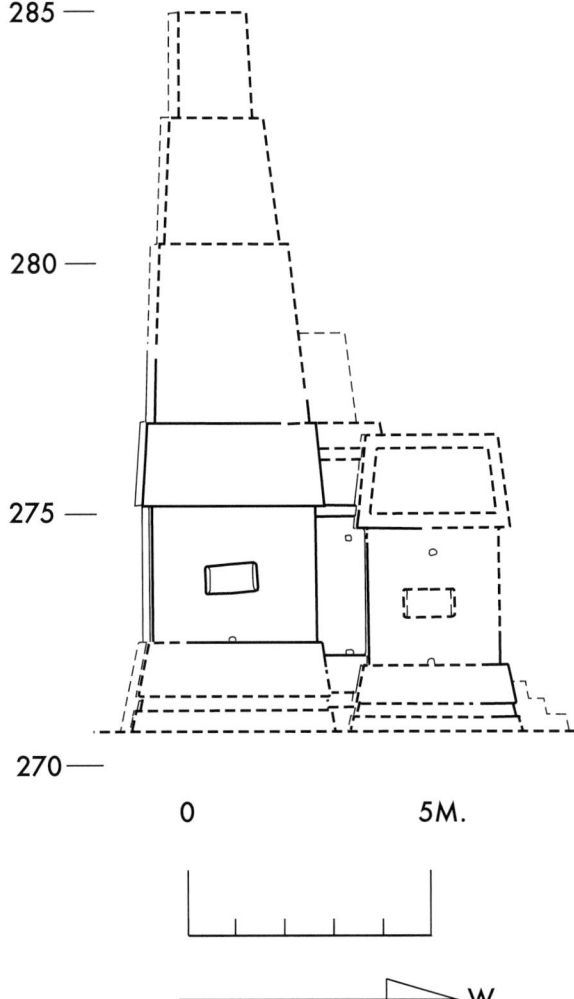

Str. 5D-87 N Elevation (scale 1:150).

FIGURE 31

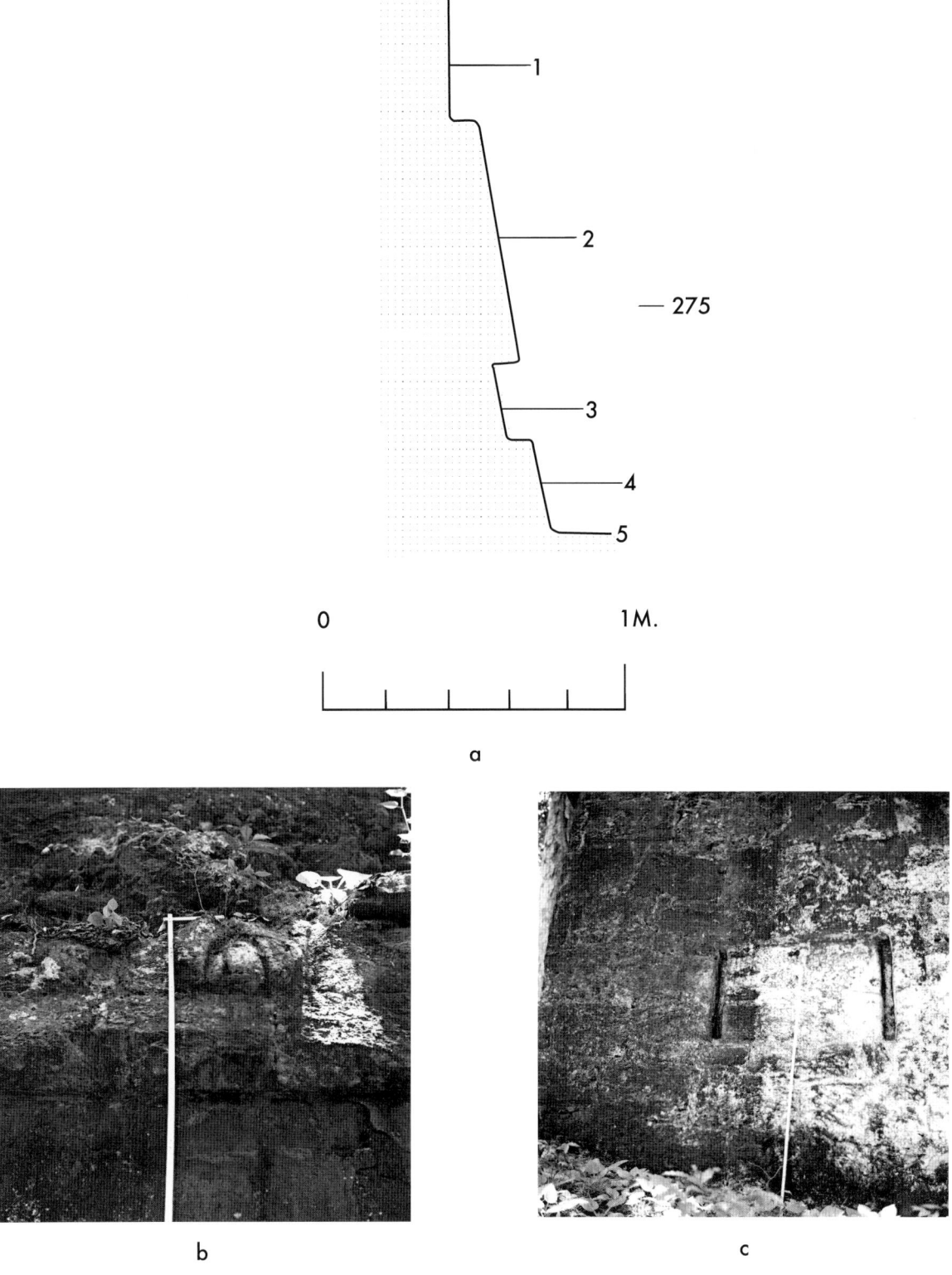

Str. 5D-87 Details.
a. Apron profile at NW corner of building platform. *1*, Exterior face of building wall. *2*, Apron. *3*, Subapron. *4*, Basal molding. *5*, Top of lower substructure platform. *b*. Sculpture fragment in rear axial upper zone. *c*. Inset panel, N facade, rear part.

FIGURE 32

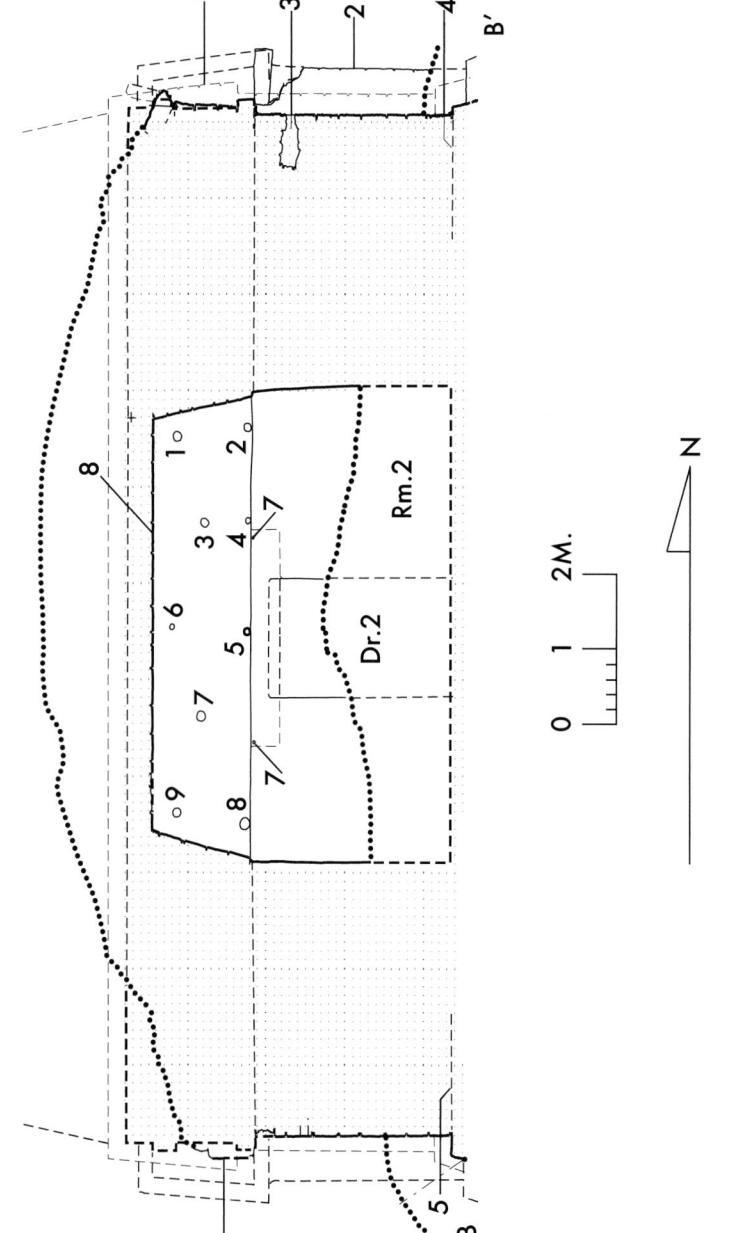

Str. 5D-87 Section/Profile B-B' (scale 1:100).
1, Profile to rear of section line. *2*, Profile in front of section line. *3*, Hole, probably animal or bird. *4*, Plaster surface, burned. *5*, Mortar surface. *6*, Displaced upper-zone material. *7*, Rod-row hole. *8*, Preplastered capstones. *1–9*, Vault-beam sockets.

FIGURE 33

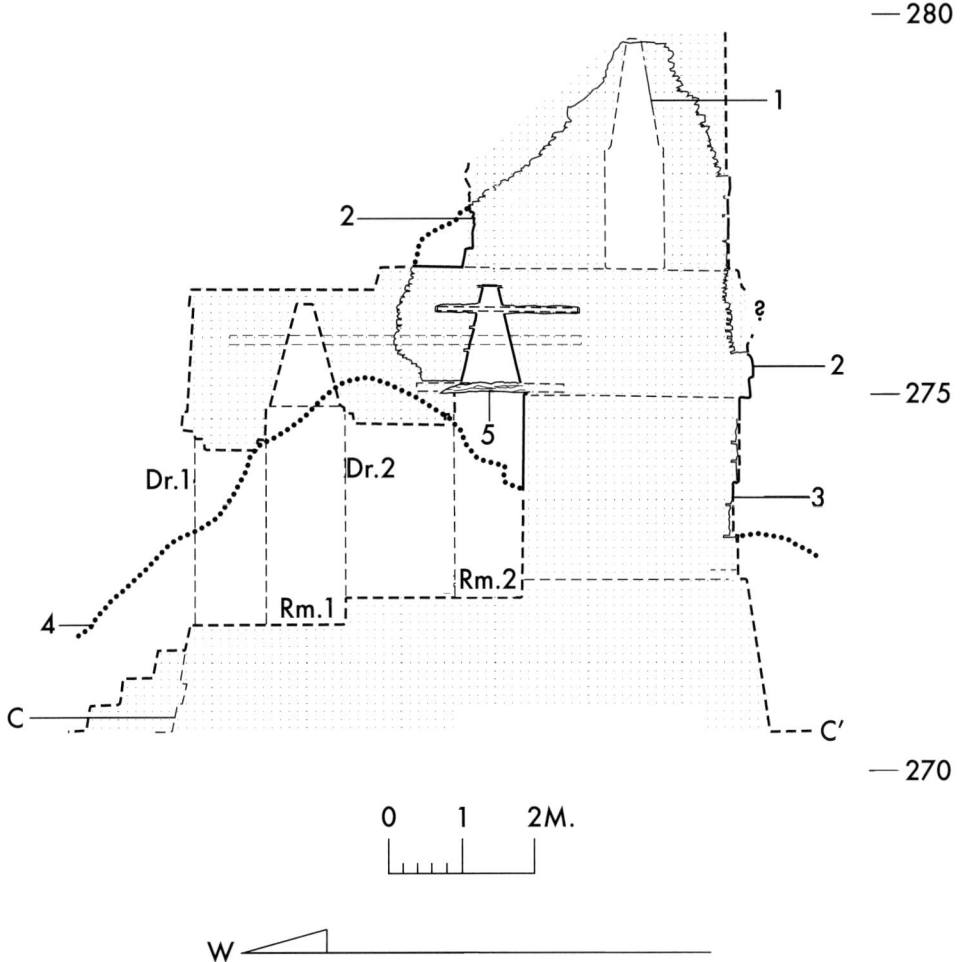

Str. 5D-87 Section/Profile C-C' (scale 1:100).
1, Vault-soffit seen off-section. *2*, Sculptural feature. *3*, Inset panel. *4*, Profile noted off-section.
5, VB. 5.

FIGURE 34

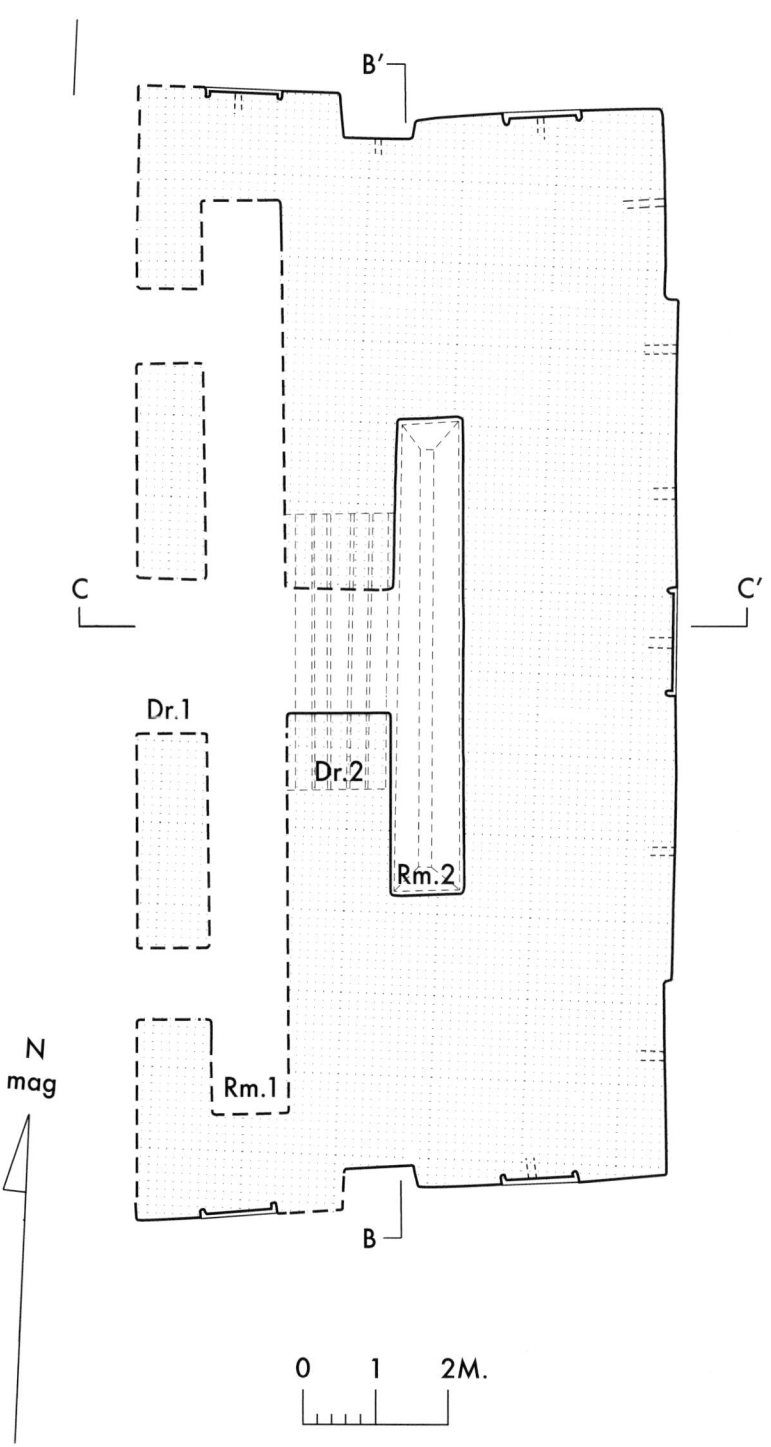

Str. 5D-87 Building Plan (scale 1:100).

FIGURE 35

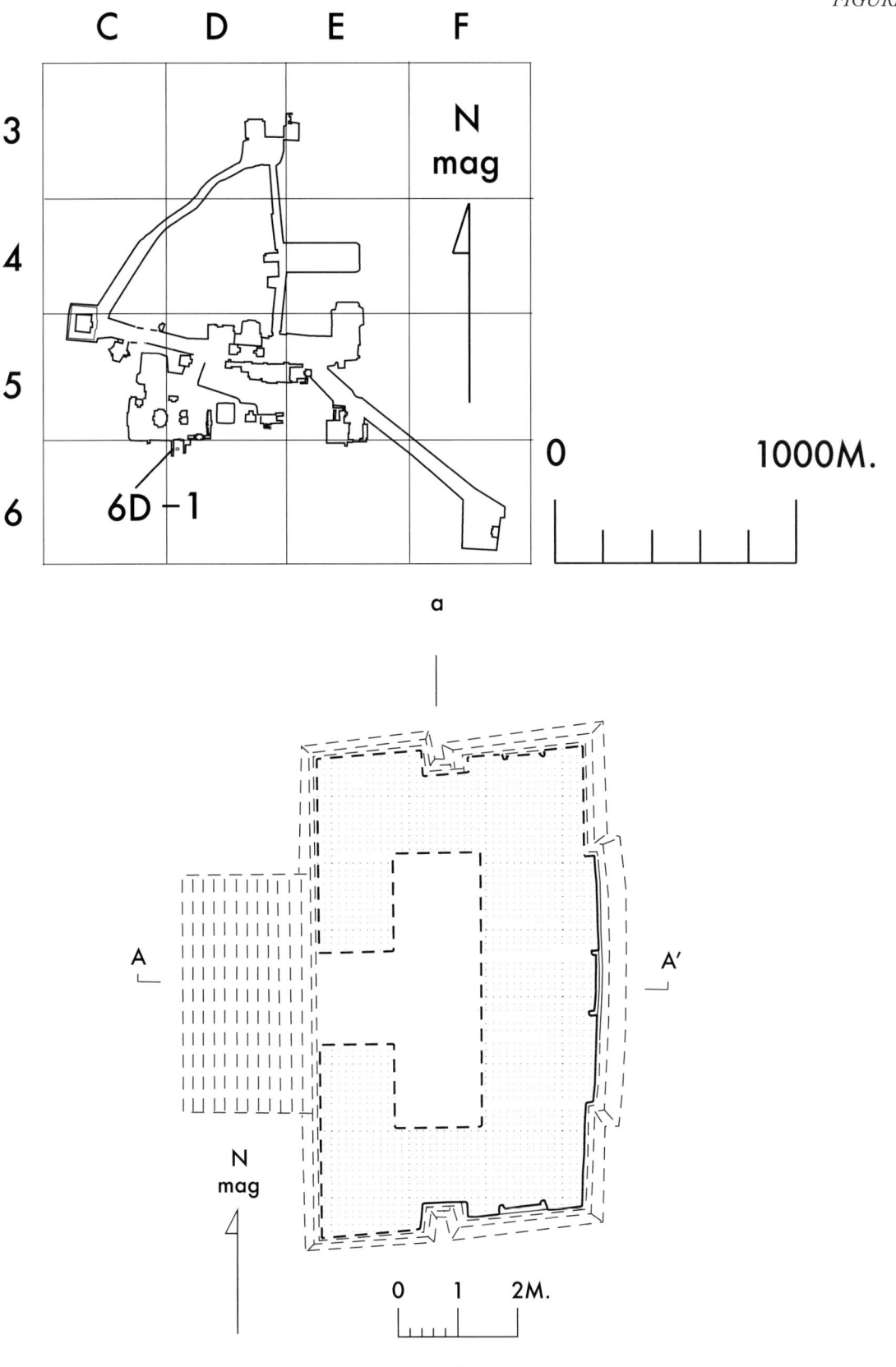

Str. 6D-1 Location and Plan.
a. Location map after TR. 11 (scale 1:25,000). *b*. Plan (scale 1:100).

FIGURE 36

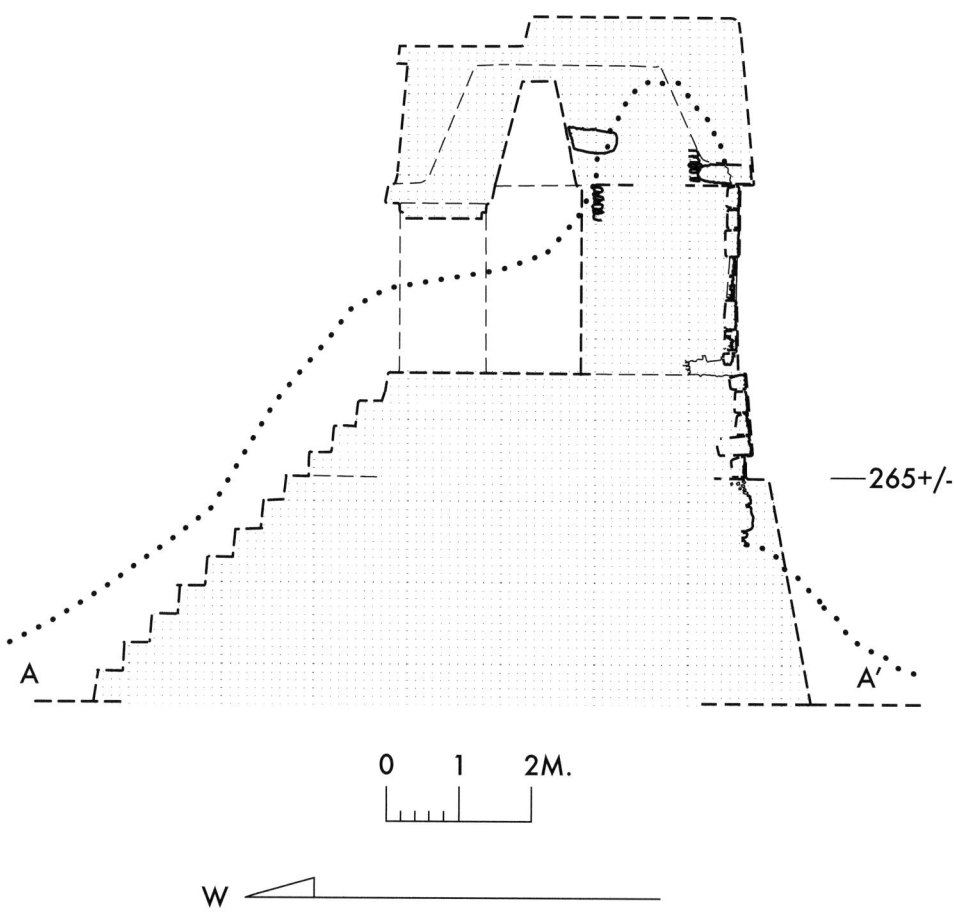

Str. 6D-1 Section/Profile A-A' (scale 1:100).